C-383 CAREER EXAMINATION SERIES

This is your
PASSBOOK for...

Park Manager I

Test Preparation Study Guide
Questions & Answers

NATIONAL LEARNING CORPORATION®

COPYRIGHT NOTICE

This book is SOLELY intended for, is sold ONLY to, and its use is RESTRICTED to individual, bona fide applicants or candidates who qualify by virtue of having seriously filed applications for appropriate license, certificate, professional and/or promotional advancement, higher school matriculation, scholarship, or other legitimate requirements of education and/or governmental authorities.

This book is NOT intended for use, class instruction, tutoring, training, duplication, copying, reprinting, excerption, or adaptation, etc., by:

1) Other publishers
2) Proprietors and/or Instructors of "Coaching" and/or Preparatory Courses
3) Personnel and/or Training Divisions of commercial, industrial, and governmental organizations
4) Schools, colleges, or universities and/or their departments and staffs, including teachers and other personnel
5) Testing Agencies or Bureaus
6) Study groups which seek by the purchase of a single volume to copy and/or duplicate and/or adapt this material for use by the group as a whole without having purchased individual volumes for each of the members of the group
7) Et al.

Such persons would be in violation of appropriate Federal and State statutes.

PROVISION OF LICENSING AGREEMENTS – Recognized educational, commercial, industrial, and governmental institutions and organizations, and others legitimately engaged in educational pursuits, including training, testing, and measurement activities, may address request for a licensing agreement to the copyright owners, who will determine whether, and under what conditions, including fees and charges, the materials in this book may be used them. In other words, a licensing facility exists for the legitimate use of the material in this book on other than an individual basis. However, it is asseverated and affirmed here that the material in this book CANNOT be used without the receipt of the express permission of such a licensing agreement from the Publishers. Inquiries re licensing should be addressed to the company, attention rights and permissions department.

All rights reserved, including the right of reproduction in whole or in part, in any form or by any means, electronic or mechanical, including photocopying, recording, or by any information storage and retrieval system, without permission in writing from the Publisher.

Copyright © 2024 by
National Learning Corporation

212 Michael Drive, Syosset, NY 11791
(516) 921-8888 • www.passbooks.com
E-mail: info@passbooks.com

PUBLISHED IN THE UNITED STATES OF AMERICA

PASSBOOK® SERIES

THE *PASSBOOK® SERIES* has been created to prepare applicants and candidates for the ultimate academic battlefield – the examination room.

At some time in our lives, each and every one of us may be required to take an examination – for validation, matriculation, admission, qualification, registration, certification, or licensure.

Based on the assumption that every applicant or candidate has met the basic formal educational standards, has taken the required number of courses, and read the necessary texts, the *PASSBOOK® SERIES* furnishes the one special preparation which may assure passing with confidence, instead of failing with insecurity. Examination questions – together with answers – are furnished as the basic vehicle for study so that the mysteries of the examination and its compounding difficulties may be eliminated or diminished by a sure method.

This book is meant to help you pass your examination provided that you qualify and are serious in your objective.

The entire field is reviewed through the huge store of content information which is succinctly presented through a provocative and challenging approach – the question-and-answer method.

A climate of success is established by furnishing the correct answers at the end of each test.

You soon learn to recognize types of questions, forms of questions, and patterns of questioning. You may even begin to anticipate expected outcomes.

You perceive that many questions are repeated or adapted so that you can gain acute insights, which may enable you to score many sure points.

You learn how to confront new questions, or types of questions, and to attack them confidently and work out the correct answers.

You note objectives and emphases, and recognize pitfalls and dangers, so that you may make positive educational adjustments.

Moreover, you are kept fully informed in relation to new concepts, methods, practices, and directions in the field.

You discover that you are actually taking the examination all the time: you are preparing for the examination by "taking" an examination, not by reading extraneous and/or supererogatory textbooks.

In short, this PASSBOOK®, used directedly, should be an important factor in helping you to pass your test.

PARK MANAGER I

DUTIES
As a Park Manager I, you would have responsibility for planning, directing and coordinating the operation, recreation programming and maintenance of all recreation facilities in a park or group of parks within a geographical region. You would supervise, direct, manage and coordinate various levels of staff in recreation, security, operation and maintenance areas.

SCOPE OF THE EXAMINATION
The written test is designed to test for knowledge, skills and/or abilities in such areas as:

1. Educating and interacting with the public;
2. Park business office management, including revenue management, budgeting, purchasing, payroll, and related internal controls;
3. Park operations, maintenance and procedures;
4. Work scheduling;
5. Preparing written material;
6. Supervision; and
7. Understanding and interpreting written material.

HOW TO TAKE A TEST

I. YOU MUST PASS AN EXAMINATION

A. *WHAT EVERY CANDIDATE SHOULD KNOW*

   Examination applicants often ask us for help in preparing for the written test. What can I study in advance? What kinds of questions will be asked? How will the test be given? How will the papers be graded?

   As an applicant for a civil service examination, you may be wondering about some of these things. Our purpose here is to suggest effective methods of advance study and to describe civil service examinations.

   Your chances for success on this examination can be increased if you know how to prepare. Those "pre-examination jitters" can be reduced if you know what to expect. You can even experience an adventure in good citizenship if you know why civil service exams are given.

B. *WHY ARE CIVIL SERVICE EXAMINATIONS GIVEN?*

   Civil service examinations are important to you in two ways. As a citizen, you want public jobs filled by employees who know how to do their work. As a job seeker, you want a fair chance to compete for that job on an equal footing with other candidates. The best-known means of accomplishing this two-fold goal is the competitive examination.

   Exams are widely publicized throughout the nation. They may be administered for jobs in federal, state, city, municipal, town or village governments or agencies.

   Any citizen may apply, with some limitations, such as the age or residence of applicants. Your experience and education may be reviewed to see whether you meet the requirements for the particular examination. When these requirements exist, they are reasonable and applied consistently to all applicants. Thus, a competitive examination may cause you some uneasiness now, but it is your privilege and safeguard.

C. *HOW ARE CIVIL SERVICE EXAMS DEVELOPED?*

   Examinations are carefully written by trained technicians who are specialists in the field known as "psychological measurement," in consultation with recognized authorities in the field of work that the test will cover. These experts recommend the subject matter areas or skills to be tested; only those knowledges or skills important to your success on the job are included. The most reliable books and source materials available are used as references. Together, the experts and technicians judge the difficulty level of the questions.

   Test technicians know how to phrase questions so that the problem is clearly stated. Their ethics do not permit "trick" or "catch" questions. Questions may have been tried out on sample groups, or subjected to statistical analysis, to determine their usefulness.

   Written tests are often used in combination with performance tests, ratings of training and experience, and oral interviews. All of these measures combine to form the best-known means of finding the right person for the right job.

II. HOW TO PASS THE WRITTEN TEST

A. NATURE OF THE EXAMINATION

To prepare intelligently for civil service examinations, you should know how they differ from school examinations you have taken. In school you were assigned certain definite pages to read or subjects to cover. The examination questions were quite detailed and usually emphasized memory. Civil service exams, on the other hand, try to discover your present ability to perform the duties of a position, plus your potentiality to learn these duties. In other words, a civil service exam attempts to predict how successful you will be. Questions cover such a broad area that they cannot be as minute and detailed as school exam questions.

In the public service similar kinds of work, or positions, are grouped together in one "class." This process is known as *position-classification*. All the positions in a class are paid according to the salary range for that class. One class title covers all of these positions, and they are all tested by the same examination.

B. FOUR BASIC STEPS

1) Study the announcement

How, then, can you know what subjects to study? Our best answer is: "Learn as much as possible about the class of positions for which you've applied." The exam will test the knowledge, skills and abilities needed to do the work.

Your most valuable source of information about the position you want is the official exam announcement. This announcement lists the training and experience qualifications. Check these standards and apply only if you come reasonably close to meeting them.

The brief description of the position in the examination announcement offers some clues to the subjects which will be tested. Think about the job itself. Review the duties in your mind. Can you perform them, or are there some in which you are rusty? Fill in the blank spots in your preparation.

Many jurisdictions preview the written test in the exam announcement by including a section called "Knowledge and Abilities Required," "Scope of the Examination," or some similar heading. Here you will find out specifically what fields will be tested.

2) Review your own background

Once you learn in general what the position is all about, and what you need to know to do the work, ask yourself which subjects you already know fairly well and which need improvement. You may wonder whether to concentrate on improving your strong areas or on building some background in your fields of weakness. When the announcement has specified "some knowledge" or "considerable knowledge," or has used adjectives like "beginning principles of…" or "advanced … methods," you can get a clue as to the number and difficulty of questions to be asked in any given field. More questions, and hence broader coverage, would be included for those subjects which are more important in the work. Now weigh your strengths and weaknesses against the job requirements and prepare accordingly.

3) Determine the level of the position

Another way to tell how intensively you should prepare is to understand the level of the job for which you are applying. Is it the entering level? In other words, is this the position in which beginners in a field of work are hired? Or is it an intermediate or advanced level? Sometimes this is indicated by such words as "Junior" or "Senior" in the class title. Other jurisdictions use Roman numerals to designate the level – Clerk I, Clerk II, for example. The word "Supervisor" sometimes appears in the title. If the level is not indicated by the title, check the description of duties. Will you be working under very close supervision, or will you have responsibility for independent decisions in this work?

4) Choose appropriate study materials

Now that you know the subjects to be examined and the relative amount of each subject to be covered, you can choose suitable study materials. For beginning level jobs, or even advanced ones, if you have a pronounced weakness in some aspect of your training, read a modern, standard textbook in that field. Be sure it is up to date and has general coverage. Such books are normally available at your library, and the librarian will be glad to help you locate one. For entry-level positions, questions of appropriate difficulty are chosen – neither highly advanced questions, nor those too simple. Such questions require careful thought but not advanced training.

If the position for which you are applying is technical or advanced, you will read more advanced, specialized material. If you are already familiar with the basic principles of your field, elementary textbooks would waste your time. Concentrate on advanced textbooks and technical periodicals. Think through the concepts and review difficult problems in your field.

These are all general sources. You can get more ideas on your own initiative, following these leads. For example, training manuals and publications of the government agency which employs workers in your field can be useful, particularly for technical and professional positions. A letter or visit to the government department involved may result in more specific study suggestions, and certainly will provide you with a more definite idea of the exact nature of the position you are seeking.

III. KINDS OF TESTS

Tests are used for purposes other than measuring knowledge and ability to perform specified duties. For some positions, it is equally important to test ability to make adjustments to new situations or to profit from training. In others, basic mental abilities not dependent on information are essential. Questions which test these things may not appear as pertinent to the duties of the position as those which test for knowledge and information. Yet they are often highly important parts of a fair examination. For very general questions, it is almost impossible to help you direct your study efforts. What we can do is to point out some of the more common of these general abilities needed in public service positions and describe some typical questions.

1) General information

Broad, general information has been found useful for predicting job success in some kinds of work. This is tested in a variety of ways, from vocabulary lists to questions about current events. Basic background in some field of work, such as sociology or economics, may be sampled in a group of questions. Often these are principles which have become familiar to most persons through exposure rather than through formal training. It is difficult to advise you how to study for these questions; being alert to the world around you is our best suggestion.

2) Verbal ability

An example of an ability needed in many positions is verbal or language ability. Verbal ability is, in brief, the ability to use and understand words. Vocabulary and grammar tests are typical measures of this ability. Reading comprehension or paragraph interpretation questions are common in many kinds of civil service tests. You are given a paragraph of written material and asked to find its central meaning.

3) **Numerical ability**

Number skills can be tested by the familiar arithmetic problem, by checking paired lists of numbers to see which are alike and which are different, or by interpreting charts and graphs. In the latter test, a graph may be printed in the test booklet which you are asked to use as the basis for answering questions.

4) **Observation**

A popular test for law-enforcement positions is the observation test. A picture is shown to you for several minutes, then taken away. Questions about the picture test your ability to observe both details and larger elements.

5) **Following directions**

In many positions in the public service, the employee must be able to carry out written instructions dependably and accurately. You may be given a chart with several columns, each column listing a variety of information. The questions require you to carry out directions involving the information given in the chart.

6) **Skills and aptitudes**

Performance tests effectively measure some manual skills and aptitudes. When the skill is one in which you are trained, such as typing or shorthand, you can practice. These tests are often very much like those given in business school or high school courses. For many of the other skills and aptitudes, however, no short-time preparation can be made. Skills and abilities natural to you or that you have developed throughout your lifetime are being tested.

Many of the general questions just described provide all the data needed to answer the questions and ask you to use your reasoning ability to find the answers. Your best preparation for these tests, as well as for tests of facts and ideas, is to be at your physical and mental best. You, no doubt, have your own methods of getting into an exam-taking mood and keeping "in shape." The next section lists some ideas on this subject.

IV. KINDS OF QUESTIONS

Only rarely is the "essay" question, which you answer in narrative form, used in civil service tests. Civil service tests are usually of the short-answer type. Full instructions for answering these questions will be given to you at the examination. But in case this is your first experience with short-answer questions and separate answer sheets, here is what you need to know:

1) Multiple-choice Questions

Most popular of the short-answer questions is the "multiple choice" or "best answer" question. It can be used, for example, to test for factual knowledge, ability to solve problems or judgment in meeting situations found at work.

A multiple-choice question is normally one of three types—

- It can begin with an incomplete statement followed by several possible endings. You are to find the one ending which *best* completes the statement, although some of the others may not be entirely wrong.
- It can also be a complete statement in the form of a question which is answered by choosing one of the statements listed.

- It can be in the form of a problem – again you select the best answer.

Here is an example of a multiple-choice question with a discussion which should give you some clues as to the method for choosing the right answer:

When an employee has a complaint about his assignment, the action which will *best* help him overcome his difficulty is to
- A. discuss his difficulty with his coworkers
- B. take the problem to the head of the organization
- C. take the problem to the person who gave him the assignment
- D. say nothing to anyone about his complaint

In answering this question, you should study each of the choices to find which is best. Consider choice "A" – Certainly an employee may discuss his complaint with fellow employees, but no change or improvement can result, and the complaint remains unresolved. Choice "B" is a poor choice since the head of the organization probably does not know what assignment you have been given, and taking your problem to him is known as "going over the head" of the supervisor. The supervisor, or person who made the assignment, is the person who can clarify it or correct any injustice. Choice "C" is, therefore, correct. To say nothing, as in choice "D," is unwise. Supervisors have and interest in knowing the problems employees are facing, and the employee is seeking a solution to his problem.

2) True/False Questions

The "true/false" or "right/wrong" form of question is sometimes used. Here a complete statement is given. Your job is to decide whether the statement is right or wrong.

SAMPLE: A roaming cell-phone call to a nearby city costs less than a non-roaming call to a distant city.

This statement is wrong, or false, since roaming calls are more expensive.

This is not a complete list of all possible question forms, although most of the others are variations of these common types. You will always get complete directions for answering questions. Be sure you understand *how* to mark your answers – ask questions until you do.

V. RECORDING YOUR ANSWERS

Computer terminals are used more and more today for many different kinds of exams.

For an examination with very few applicants, you may be told to record your answers in the test booklet itself. Separate answer sheets are much more common. If this separate answer sheet is to be scored by machine – and this is often the case – it is highly important that you mark your answers correctly in order to get credit.

An electronic scoring machine is often used in civil service offices because of the speed with which papers can be scored. Machine-scored answer sheets must be marked with a pencil, which will be given to you. This pencil has a high graphite content which responds to the electronic scoring machine. As a matter of fact, stray dots may register as answers, so do not let your pencil rest on the answer sheet while you are pondering the correct answer. Also, if your pencil lead breaks or is otherwise defective, ask for another.

Since the answer sheet will be dropped in a slot in the scoring machine, be careful not to bend the corners or get the paper crumpled.

The answer sheet normally has five vertical columns of numbers, with 30 numbers to a column. These numbers correspond to the question numbers in your test booklet. After each number, going across the page are four or five pairs of dotted lines. These short dotted lines have small letters or numbers above them. The first two pairs may also have a "T" or "F" above the letters. This indicates that the first two pairs only are to be used if the questions are of the true-false type. If the questions are multiple choice, disregard the "T" and "F" and pay attention only to the small letters or numbers.

Answer your questions in the manner of the sample that follows:

32. The largest city in the United States is
    A. Washington, D.C.
    B. New York City
    C. Chicago
    D. Detroit
    E. San Francisco

1) Choose the answer you think is best. (New York City is the largest, so "B" is correct.)
2) Find the row of dotted lines numbered the same as the question you are answering. (Find row number 32)
3) Find the pair of dotted lines corresponding to the answer. (Find the pair of lines under the mark "B.")
4) Make a solid black mark between the dotted lines.

VI. BEFORE THE TEST

Common sense will help you find procedures to follow to get ready for an examination. Too many of us, however, overlook these sensible measures. Indeed, nervousness and fatigue have been found to be the most serious reasons why applicants fail to do their best on civil service tests. Here is a list of reminders:

- Begin your preparation early – Don't wait until the last minute to go scurrying around for books and materials or to find out what the position is all about.
- Prepare continuously – An hour a night for a week is better than an all-night cram session. This has been definitely established. What is more, a night a week for a month will return better dividends than crowding your study into a shorter period of time.
- Locate the place of the exam – You have been sent a notice telling you when and where to report for the examination. If the location is in a different town or otherwise unfamiliar to you, it would be well to inquire the best route and learn something about the building.
- Relax the night before the test – Allow your mind to rest. Do not study at all that night. Plan some mild recreation or diversion; then go to bed early and get a good night's sleep.
- Get up early enough to make a leisurely trip to the place for the test – This way unforeseen events, traffic snarls, unfamiliar buildings, etc. will not upset you.
- Dress comfortably – A written test is not a fashion show. You will be known by number and not by name, so wear something comfortable.

- Leave excess paraphernalia at home – Shopping bags and odd bundles will get in your way. You need bring only the items mentioned in the official notice you received; usually everything you need is provided. Do not bring reference books to the exam. They will only confuse those last minutes and be taken away from you when in the test room.
- Arrive somewhat ahead of time – If because of transportation schedules you must get there very early, bring a newspaper or magazine to take your mind off yourself while waiting.
- Locate the examination room – When you have found the proper room, you will be directed to the seat or part of the room where you will sit. Sometimes you are given a sheet of instructions to read while you are waiting. Do not fill out any forms until you are told to do so; just read them and be prepared.
- Relax and prepare to listen to the instructions
- If you have any physical problem that may keep you from doing your best, be sure to tell the test administrator. If you are sick or in poor health, you really cannot do your best on the exam. You can come back and take the test some other time.

VII. AT THE TEST

The day of the test is here and you have the test booklet in your hand. The temptation to get going is very strong. Caution! There is more to success than knowing the right answers. You must know how to identify your papers and understand variations in the type of short-answer question used in this particular examination. Follow these suggestions for maximum results from your efforts:

1) Cooperate with the monitor

The test administrator has a duty to create a situation in which you can be as much at ease as possible. He will give instructions, tell you when to begin, check to see that you are marking your answer sheet correctly, and so on. He is not there to guard you, although he will see that your competitors do not take unfair advantage. He wants to help you do your best.

2) Listen to all instructions

Don't jump the gun! Wait until you understand all directions. In most civil service tests you get more time than you need to answer the questions. So don't be in a hurry. Read each word of instructions until you clearly understand the meaning. Study the examples, listen to all announcements and follow directions. Ask questions if you do not understand what to do.

3) Identify your papers

Civil service exams are usually identified by number only. You will be assigned a number; you must not put your name on your test papers. Be sure to copy your number correctly. Since more than one exam may be given, copy your exact examination title.

4) Plan your time

Unless you are told that a test is a "speed" or "rate of work" test, speed itself is usually not important. Time enough to answer all the questions will be provided, but this does not mean that you have all day. An overall time limit has been set. Divide the total time (in minutes) by the number of questions to determine the approximate time you have for each question.

5) Do not linger over difficult questions

If you come across a difficult question, mark it with a paper clip (useful to have along) and come back to it when you have been through the booklet. One caution if you do this – be sure to skip a number on your answer sheet as well. Check often to be sure that you have not lost your place and that you are marking in the row numbered the same as the question you are answering.

6) Read the questions

Be sure you know what the question asks! Many capable people are unsuccessful because they failed to *read* the questions correctly.

7) Answer all questions

Unless you have been instructed that a penalty will be deducted for incorrect answers, it is better to guess than to omit a question.

8) Speed tests

It is often better NOT to guess on speed tests. It has been found that on timed tests people are tempted to spend the last few seconds before time is called in marking answers at random – without even reading them – in the hope of picking up a few extra points. To discourage this practice, the instructions may warn you that your score will be "corrected" for guessing. That is, a penalty will be applied. The incorrect answers will be deducted from the correct ones, or some other penalty formula will be used.

9) Review your answers

If you finish before time is called, go back to the questions you guessed or omitted to give them further thought. Review other answers if you have time.

10) Return your test materials

If you are ready to leave before others have finished or time is called, take ALL your materials to the monitor and leave quietly. Never take any test material with you. The monitor can discover whose papers are not complete, and taking a test booklet may be grounds for disqualification.

VIII. EXAMINATION TECHNIQUES

1) Read the general instructions carefully. These are usually printed on the first page of the exam booklet. As a rule, these instructions refer to the timing of the examination; the fact that you should not start work until the signal and must stop work at a signal, etc. If there are any *special* instructions, such as a choice of questions to be answered, make sure that you note this instruction carefully.

2) When you are ready to start work on the examination, that is as soon as the signal has been given, read the instructions to each question booklet, underline any key words or phrases, such as *least, best, outline, describe* and the like. In this way you will tend to answer as requested rather than discover on reviewing your paper that you *listed without describing*, that you selected the *worst* choice rather than the *best* choice, etc.

3) If the examination is of the objective or multiple-choice type – that is, each question will also give a series of possible answers: A, B, C or D, and you are called upon to select the best answer and write the letter next to that answer on your answer paper – it is advisable to start answering each question in turn. There may be anywhere from 50 to 100 such questions in the three or four hours allotted and you can see how much time would be taken if you read through all the questions before beginning to answer any. Furthermore, if you come across a question or group of questions which you know would be difficult to answer, it would undoubtedly affect your handling of all the other questions.

4) If the examination is of the essay type and contains but a few questions, it is a moot point as to whether you should read all the questions before starting to answer any one. Of course, if you are given a choice – say five out of seven and the like – then it is essential to read all the questions so you can eliminate the two that are most difficult. If, however, you are asked to answer all the questions, there may be danger in trying to answer the easiest one first because you may find that you will spend too much time on it. The best technique is to answer the first question, then proceed to the second, etc.

5) Time your answers. Before the exam begins, write down the time it started, then add the time allowed for the examination and write down the time it must be completed, then divide the time available somewhat as follows:
    - If 3-1/2 hours are allowed, that would be 210 minutes. If you have 80 objective-type questions, that would be an average of 2-1/2 minutes per question. Allow yourself no more than 2 minutes per question, or a total of 160 minutes, which will permit about 50 minutes to review.
    - If for the time allotment of 210 minutes there are 7 essay questions to answer, that would average about 30 minutes a question. Give yourself only 25 minutes per question so that you have about 35 minutes to review.

6) The most important instruction is to *read each question* and make sure you know what is wanted. The second most important instruction is to *time yourself properly* so that you answer every question. The third most important instruction is to *answer every question*. Guess if you have to but include something for each question. Remember that you will receive no credit for a blank and will probably receive some credit if you write something in answer to an essay question. If you guess a letter – say "B" for a multiple-choice question – you may have guessed right. If you leave a blank as an answer to a multiple-choice question, the examiners may respect your feelings but it will not add a point to your score. Some exams may penalize you for wrong answers, so in such cases *only*, you may not want to guess unless you have some basis for your answer.

7) Suggestions
   a. Objective-type questions
      1. Examine the question booklet for proper sequence of pages and questions
      2. Read all instructions carefully
      3. Skip any question which seems too difficult; return to it after all other questions have been answered
      4. Apportion your time properly; do not spend too much time on any single question or group of questions

5. Note and underline key words – *all, most, fewest, least, best, worst, same, opposite*, etc.
6. Pay particular attention to negatives
7. Note unusual option, e.g., unduly long, short, complex, different or similar in content to the body of the question
8. Observe the use of "hedging" words – *probably, may, most likely*, etc.
9. Make sure that your answer is put next to the same number as the question
10. Do not second-guess unless you have good reason to believe the second answer is definitely more correct
11. Cross out original answer if you decide another answer is more accurate; do not erase until you are ready to hand your paper in
12. Answer all questions; guess unless instructed otherwise
13. Leave time for review

b. Essay questions
1. Read each question carefully
2. Determine exactly what is wanted. Underline key words or phrases.
3. Decide on outline or paragraph answer
4. Include many different points and elements unless asked to develop any one or two points or elements
5. Show impartiality by giving pros and cons unless directed to select one side only
6. Make and write down any assumptions you find necessary to answer the questions
7. Watch your English, grammar, punctuation and choice of words
8. Time your answers; don't crowd material

8) Answering the essay question

Most essay questions can be answered by framing the specific response around several key words or ideas. Here are a few such key words or ideas:

M's: manpower, materials, methods, money, management
P's: purpose, program, policy, plan, procedure, practice, problems, pitfalls, personnel, public relations

a. Six basic steps in handling problems:
1. Preliminary plan and background development
2. Collect information, data and facts
3. Analyze and interpret information, data and facts
4. Analyze and develop solutions as well as make recommendations
5. Prepare report and sell recommendations
6. Install recommendations and follow up effectiveness

b. Pitfalls to avoid
1. *Taking things for granted* – A statement of the situation does not necessarily imply that each of the elements is necessarily true; for example, a complaint may be invalid and biased so that all that can be taken for granted is that a complaint has been registered

2. *Considering only one side of a situation* – Wherever possible, indicate several alternatives and then point out the reasons you selected the best one
3. *Failing to indicate follow up* – Whenever your answer indicates action on your part, make certain that you will take proper follow-up action to see how successful your recommendations, procedures or actions turn out to be
4. *Taking too long in answering any single question* – Remember to time your answers properly

IX. AFTER THE TEST

Scoring procedures differ in detail among civil service jurisdictions although the general principles are the same. Whether the papers are hand-scored or graded by machine we have described, they are nearly always graded by number. That is, the person who marks the paper knows only the number – never the name – of the applicant. Not until all the papers have been graded will they be matched with names. If other tests, such as training and experience or oral interview ratings have been given, scores will be combined. Different parts of the examination usually have different weights. For example, the written test might count 60 percent of the final grade, and a rating of training and experience 40 percent. In many jurisdictions, veterans will have a certain number of points added to their grades.

After the final grade has been determined, the names are placed in grade order and an eligible list is established. There are various methods for resolving ties between those who get the same final grade – probably the most common is to place first the name of the person whose application was received first. Job offers are made from the eligible list in the order the names appear on it. You will be notified of your grade and your rank as soon as all these computations have been made. This will be done as rapidly as possible.

People who are found to meet the requirements in the announcement are called "eligibles." Their names are put on a list of eligible candidates. An eligible's chances of getting a job depend on how high he stands on this list and how fast agencies are filling jobs from the list.

When a job is to be filled from a list of eligibles, the agency asks for the names of people on the list of eligibles for that job. When the civil service commission receives this request, it sends to the agency the names of the three people highest on this list. Or, if the job to be filled has specialized requirements, the office sends the agency the names of the top three persons who meet these requirements from the general list.

The appointing officer makes a choice from among the three people whose names were sent to him. If the selected person accepts the appointment, the names of the others are put back on the list to be considered for future openings.

That is the rule in hiring from all kinds of eligible lists, whether they are for typist, carpenter, chemist, or something else. For every vacancy, the appointing officer has his choice of any one of the top three eligibles on the list. This explains why the person whose name is on top of the list sometimes does not get an appointment when some of the persons lower on the list do. If the appointing officer chooses the second or third eligible, the No. 1 eligible does not get a job at once, but stays on the list until he is appointed or the list is terminated.

X. HOW TO PASS THE INTERVIEW TEST

The examination for which you applied requires an oral interview test. You have already taken the written test and you are now being called for the interview test – the final part of the formal examination.

You may think that it is not possible to prepare for an interview test and that there are no procedures to follow during an interview. Our purpose is to point out some things you can do in advance that will help you and some good rules to follow and pitfalls to avoid while you are being interviewed.

What is an interview supposed to test?

The written examination is designed to test the technical knowledge and competence of the candidate; the oral is designed to evaluate intangible qualities, not readily measured otherwise, and to establish a list showing the relative fitness of each candidate – as measured against his competitors – for the position sought. Scoring is not on the basis of "right" and "wrong," but on a sliding scale of values ranging from "not passable" to "outstanding." As a matter of fact, it is possible to achieve a relatively low score without a single "incorrect" answer because of evident weakness in the qualities being measured.

Occasionally, an examination may consist entirely of an oral test – either an individual or a group oral. In such cases, information is sought concerning the technical knowledges and abilities of the candidate, since there has been no written examination for this purpose. More commonly, however, an oral test is used to supplement a written examination.

Who conducts interviews?

The composition of oral boards varies among different jurisdictions. In nearly all, a representative of the personnel department serves as chairman. One of the members of the board may be a representative of the department in which the candidate would work. In some cases, "outside experts" are used, and, frequently, a businessman or some other representative of the general public is asked to serve. Labor and management or other special groups may be represented. The aim is to secure the services of experts in the appropriate field.

However the board is composed, it is a good idea (and not at all improper or unethical) to ascertain in advance of the interview who the members are and what groups they represent. When you are introduced to them, you will have some idea of their backgrounds and interests, and at least you will not stutter and stammer over their names.

What should be done before the interview?

While knowledge about the board members is useful and takes some of the surprise element out of the interview, there is other preparation which is more substantive. It *is* possible to prepare for an oral interview – in several ways:

1) Keep a copy of your application and review it carefully before the interview

This may be the only document before the oral board, and the starting point of the interview. Know what education and experience you have listed there, and the sequence and dates of all of it. Sometimes the board will ask you to review the highlights of your experience for them; you should not have to hem and haw doing it.

2) Study the class specification and the examination announcement

Usually, the oral board has one or both of these to guide them. The qualities, characteristics or knowledges required by the position sought are stated in these documents. They offer valuable clues as to the nature of the oral interview. For example, if the job involves supervisory responsibilities, the announcement will usually indicate that knowledge of modern supervisory methods and the qualifications of the candidate as a supervisor will be tested. If so, you can expect such questions, frequently in the form of a hypothetical situation which you are expected to solve. NEVER go into an oral without knowledge of the duties and responsibilities of the job you seek.

3) Think through each qualification required

Try to visualize the kind of questions you would ask if you were a board member. How well could you answer them? Try especially to appraise your own knowledge and background in each area, *measured against the job sought*, and identify any areas in which you are weak. Be critical and realistic – do not flatter yourself.

4) Do some general reading in areas in which you feel you may be weak

For example, if the job involves supervision and your past experience has NOT, some general reading in supervisory methods and practices, particularly in the field of human relations, might be useful. Do NOT study agency procedures or detailed manuals. The oral board will be testing your understanding and capacity, not your memory.

5) Get a good night's sleep and watch your general health and mental attitude

You will want a clear head at the interview. Take care of a cold or any other minor ailment, and of course, no hangovers.

What should be done on the day of the interview?

Now comes the day of the interview itself. Give yourself plenty of time to get there. Plan to arrive somewhat ahead of the scheduled time, particularly if your appointment is in the fore part of the day. If a previous candidate fails to appear, the board might be ready for you a bit early. By early afternoon an oral board is almost invariably behind schedule if there are many candidates, and you may have to wait. Take along a book or magazine to read, or your application to review, but leave any extraneous material in the waiting room when you go in for your interview. In any event, relax and compose yourself.

The matter of dress is important. The board is forming impressions about you – from your experience, your manners, your attitude, and your appearance. Give your personal appearance careful attention. Dress your best, but not your flashiest. Choose conservative, appropriate clothing, and be sure it is immaculate. This is a business interview, and your appearance should indicate that you regard it as such. Besides, being well groomed and properly dressed will help boost your confidence.

Sooner or later, someone will call your name and escort you into the interview room. *This is it.* From here on you are on your own. It is too late for any more preparation. But remember, you asked for this opportunity to prove your fitness, and you are here because your request was granted.

What happens when you go in?

The usual sequence of events will be as follows: The clerk (who is often the board stenographer) will introduce you to the chairman of the oral board, who will introduce you to the other members of the board. Acknowledge the introductions before you sit down. Do not be surprised if you find a microphone facing you or a stenotypist sitting by. Oral interviews are usually recorded in the event of an appeal or other review.

Usually the chairman of the board will open the interview by reviewing the highlights of your education and work experience from your application – primarily for the benefit of the other members of the board, as well as to get the material into the record. Do not interrupt or comment unless there is an error or significant misinterpretation; if that is the case, do not hesitate. But do not quibble about insignificant matters. Also, he will usually ask you some question about your education, experience or your present job – partly to get you to start talking and to establish the interviewing "rapport." He may start the actual questioning, or turn it over to one of the other members. Frequently, each member undertakes the questioning on a particular area, one in which he is perhaps most competent, so you can expect each member to participate in the examination. Because time is limited, you may also expect some rather abrupt switches in the direction the questioning takes, so do not be upset by it. Normally, a board member will not pursue a single line of questioning unless he discovers a particular strength or weakness.

After each member has participated, the chairman will usually ask whether any member has any further questions, then will ask you if you have anything you wish to add. Unless you are expecting this question, it may floor you. Worse, it may start you off on an extended, extemporaneous speech. The board is not usually seeking more information. The question is principally to offer you a last opportunity to present further qualifications or to indicate that you have nothing to add. So, if you feel that a significant qualification or characteristic has been overlooked, it is proper to point it out in a sentence or so. Do not compliment the board on the thoroughness of their examination – they have been sketchy, and you know it. If you wish, merely say, "No thank you, I have nothing further to add." This is a point where you can "talk yourself out" of a good impression or fail to present an important bit of information. Remember, *you close the interview yourself.*

The chairman will then say, "That is all, Mr. _____, thank you." Do not be startled; the interview is over, and quicker than you think. Thank him, gather your belongings and take your leave. Save your sigh of relief for the other side of the door.

How to put your best foot forward

Throughout this entire process, you may feel that the board individually and collectively is trying to pierce your defenses, seek out your hidden weaknesses and embarrass and confuse you. Actually, this is not true. They are obliged to make an appraisal of your qualifications for the job you are seeking, and they want to see you in your best light. Remember, they must interview all candidates and a non-cooperative candidate may become a failure in spite of their best efforts to bring out his qualifications. Here are 15 suggestions that will help you:

1) Be natural – Keep your attitude confident, not cocky

If you are not confident that you can do the job, do not expect the board to be. Do not apologize for your weaknesses, try to bring out your strong points. The board is interested in a positive, not negative, presentation. Cockiness will antagonize any board member and make him wonder if you are covering up a weakness by a false show of strength.

2) Get comfortable, but don't lounge or sprawl

Sit erectly but not stiffly. A careless posture may lead the board to conclude that you are careless in other things, or at least that you are not impressed by the importance of the occasion. Either conclusion is natural, even if incorrect. Do not fuss with your clothing, a pencil or an ashtray. Your hands may occasionally be useful to emphasize a point; do not let them become a point of distraction.

3) Do not wisecrack or make small talk

This is a serious situation, and your attitude should show that you consider it as such. Further, the time of the board is limited – they do not want to waste it, and neither should you.

4) Do not exaggerate your experience or abilities
In the first place, from information in the application or other interviews and sources, the board may know more about you than you think. Secondly, you probably will not get away with it. An experienced board is rather adept at spotting such a situation, so do not take the chance.

5) If you know a board member, do not make a point of it, yet do not hide it
Certainly you are not fooling him, and probably not the other members of the board. Do not try to take advantage of your acquaintanceship – it will probably do you little good.

6) Do not dominate the interview
Let the board do that. They will give you the clues – do not assume that you have to do all the talking. Realize that the board has a number of questions to ask you, and do not try to take up all the interview time by showing off your extensive knowledge of the answer to the first one.

7) Be attentive
You only have 20 minutes or so, and you should keep your attention at its sharpest throughout. When a member is addressing a problem or question to you, give him your undivided attention. Address your reply principally to him, but do not exclude the other board members.

8) Do not interrupt
A board member may be stating a problem for you to analyze. He will ask you a question when the time comes. Let him state the problem, and wait for the question.

9) Make sure you understand the question
Do not try to answer until you are sure what the question is. If it is not clear, restate it in your own words or ask the board member to clarify it for you. However, do not haggle about minor elements.

10) Reply promptly but not hastily
A common entry on oral board rating sheets is "candidate responded readily," or "candidate hesitated in replies." Respond as promptly and quickly as you can, but do not jump to a hasty, ill-considered answer.

11) Do not be peremptory in your answers
A brief answer is proper – but do not fire your answer back. That is a losing game from your point of view. The board member can probably ask questions much faster than you can answer them.

12) Do not try to create the answer you think the board member wants
He is interested in what kind of mind you have and how it works – not in playing games. Furthermore, he can usually spot this practice and will actually grade you down on it.

13) Do not switch sides in your reply merely to agree with a board member
Frequently, a member will take a contrary position merely to draw you out and to see if you are willing and able to defend your point of view. Do not start a debate, yet do not surrender a good position. If a position is worth taking, it is worth defending.

14) Do not be afraid to admit an error in judgment if you are shown to be wrong

The board knows that you are forced to reply without any opportunity for careful consideration. Your answer may be demonstrably wrong. If so, admit it and get on with the interview.

15) Do not dwell at length on your present job

The opening question may relate to your present assignment. Answer the question but do not go into an extended discussion. You are being examined for a *new* job, not your present one. As a matter of fact, try to phrase ALL your answers in terms of the job for which you are being examined.

Basis of Rating

Probably you will forget most of these "do's" and "don'ts" when you walk into the oral interview room. Even remembering them all will not ensure you a passing grade. Perhaps you did not have the qualifications in the first place. But remembering them will help you to put your best foot forward, without treading on the toes of the board members.

Rumor and popular opinion to the contrary notwithstanding, an oral board wants you to make the best appearance possible. They know you are under pressure – but they also want to see how you respond to it as a guide to what your reaction would be under the pressures of the job you seek. They will be influenced by the degree of poise you display, the personal traits you show and the manner in which you respond.

ABOUT THIS BOOK

This book contains tests divided into Examination Sections. Go through each test, answering every question in the margin. We have also attached a sample answer sheet at the back of the book that can be removed and used. At the end of each test look at the answer key and check your answers. On the ones you got wrong, look at the right answer choice and learn. Do not fill in the answers first. Do not memorize the questions and answers, but understand the answer and principles involved. On your test, the questions will likely be different from the samples. Questions are changed and new ones added. If you understand these past questions you should have success with any changes that arise. Tests may consist of several types of questions. We have additional books on each subject should more study be advisable or necessary for you. Finally, the more you study, the better prepared you will be. This book is intended to be the last thing you study before you walk into the examination room. Prior study of relevant texts is also recommended. NLC publishes some of these in our Fundamental Series. Knowledge and good sense are important factors in passing your exam. Good luck also helps. So now study this Passbook, absorb the material contained within and take that knowledge into the examination. Then do your best to pass that exam.

EXAMINATION SECTION

EXAMINATION SECTION
TEST 1

DIRECTIONS: Each question or incomplete statement is followed by several suggested answers or completions. Select the one that BEST answers the question or completes the statement. *PRINT THE LETTER OF THE CORRECT ANSWER IN THE SPACE AT THE RIGHT.*

1. The basic design of neighborhood playgrounds provides for a variety of separate areas. The LARGEST of these areas in a neighborhood playground is that generally set aside for use by

    A. little children and their guardians
    B. older children, teenagers, and young adults
    C. older people (senior citizens)
    D. physically active and mature adults

    1.____

2. If a general park foreman is vague and indefinite in assigning to employees responsibilities for various phases of work, the MOST important consequence of this is likely to be

    A. a shift in lines of authority within the organization
    B. friction, misunderstanding, and ineffective work
    C. that certain more aggressive individuals will assume responsibility in order to get the work done
    D. the unsupervised and unplanned training of individuals in assuming responsibility

    2.____

3. Present recreation programs must be expanded to provide a progression of sports competition.
According to a park department report, the PRINCIPAL reason for this expanded program is the need to

    A. channel the naturally aggressive inclinations of youngsters into wholesome physical exercise and rivalry
    B. enable qualified, eligible city youths to achieve success in professional athletic activity
    C. make the fullest possible use of presently existing facilities
    D. provide the means for improving the physical fitness of male youths as a factor in national defense

    3.____

4. Aside from the requirements of law, the BASIC reason why the park department publishes periodic reports should be to

    A. emphasize the need for additional funds if it is to perform its work adequately
    B. help the public gain an understanding of its program and to try to enlist public support
    C. point up the present efficiency and the expanding responsibilities of the park department
    D. show just how the park department uses the funds it is allotted in its budget

    4.____

5. If a supervising park foreman assigns an assistant gardener to temporarily supervise a group of seasonal employees, it would be MOST important for the general park foreman to describe carefully to the assistant gardener

    5.____

A. the educational and work background of each of the seasonal employees involved
B. the length of time the assignment is likely to last
C. the nature and extent of the supervisory duties to be assumed
D. why seasonal employees are never as industrious as regular employees

6. As stated in a park department publication, the prime concern of the park department must continue to be that of

   A. developing large-scale ocean and bay front bathing and boating facilities
   B. expanding the scope of operation and varieties of services of the city's cultural institutions
   C. meeting the recreational needs of senior citizens
   D. providing adequate recreational facilities in local areas

7. Requests for information from the comptroller about claims against the city arising from accidents in the parks sometimes concern the date of the request for repairs and the date of repairs.
   This information is important in such cases MAINLY because it

   A. indicates the claimant failed to use due care in the use of park facilities
   B. is an additional check on the operation of the main tenance forces
   C. may affect the liability of the city in the accident
   D. points up the shortage of personnel available to make repairs

8. It is important for a supervisor to take prompt action upon requests from subordinates MAINLY because

   A. delays in making decisions mean that they must then be made on the basis of facts which can no longer be up-to-date
   B. favorable action on such requests is more likely to result when a decision is made quickly
   C. it is an indication that the supervisor has his work well organized
   D. promptness in such matters helps maintain good employee morale

9. As a supervisor, you realize that your superior, when under pressure, has a habit of giving you oral orders which are not always clear and also lack sufficient detail. The BEST procedure for you to follow in such situations would be to

   A. obtain clarification by requesting needed details at the time you receive such orders
   B. consider past orders of a similar nature to determine the probable intent of your superior
   C. frequently consult your superior during the course of the job in order to secure the required details to complete the job
   D. request your superior to put all his orders to you in writing

10. Some supervisors have their subordinates meet with them in group discussions of troublesome problems.
    The MAIN advantage of such group discussions as a supervisory tool is that they can be directed toward the

    A. appraisal of the personalities involved
    B. development of new policies and regulations

C. circulation of new material and information
D. pooling of experience in the solution of common problems

11. The PRINCIPAL disadvantage of using form letters to reply to written complaints made by members of the park-using public is that such form letters

    A. tend to make any investigation of the original complaint rather superficial
    B. are limited by their design to handle only a few possible situations that could give rise to complaints
    C. lack the desirable element of the personal touch for the recipient
    D. tend to lose their effectiveness by quickly becoming obsolete

12. Below are repair items in a county staff inspection report of an inspection of a large recreation center made in mid-November.
    The item for which the target date would MOST probably read *at once* would be

    A. chip, red lead and paint wrought iron fence
    B. clean one filter in kitchen exhaust duct of Golden Age Center kitchen
    C. repair broken game tables
    D. replace corktiles on swimming pool wall

13. In a headquarters inspection report, the one of the following tasks whose accomplishment would MOST probably be the responsibility of the county director is

    A. accelerating repairs to gate hinges
    B. alerting local Police Precinct and Youth Squad of exceptional vandalism
    C. replacing missing privet along Avenue S
    D. studying removal of horseshoe courts and developing same as passive recreation area

14. According to the work count report, the one of the following work units which is measured in terms of area is

    A. catch basins - hand cleaned
    B. painting - wrought iron fencing
    C. paper picking
    D. sweeping mechanically

15. A helper who has been on the job for some time complains to a foreman that he is learning very little because the maintainer with whom he works does not explain anything. The FIRST thing the foreman should do is to

    A. tell the helper to make a formal written request for a transfer
    B. send a memo to his maintainers reminding them of their responsibility to train helpers
    C. discuss the problem privately with the maintainer in question
    D. tell the helper to learn as much as he can on his own

16. With respect to the city's employee grievance procedure, it would be MOST correct to state that

A. the commissioner of labor is the highest ranking official, excepting the judge, who can be involved in a particular grievance
B. the person with the grievance has the right to be represented by virtually anyone he chooses
C. the one having the grievance (the grievant) can be represented by the majority organization only if he is a member thereof
D. time limits are not set concerning adjudication in order to insure the fullest consideration of the particular grievance

17. According to the rules and regulations of the department of parks, loitering or remaining in any park without general or special permission from the park commissioner is prohibited between

    A. 12:00 P.M. and sunrise
    B. 11:00 P.M. and one-half hour before sunrise
    C. 12:00 midnight and one-half hour before sunrise
    D. three hours after sunset and one-half hour before sunrise

17._____

18. According to the rules and regulations of the department of parks, when a sidewalk fronts on the roadway of a park-street, dust from such sidewalk may

    A. be swept into the gutter before nine o'clock in the morning
    B. be swept into the gutter, and there piled, before the first sweeping of the roadway of the park-street by the street cleaners
    C. be swept into the gutter in neat piles at any reasonable time if not so piled as to constitute a traffic hazard or health menace
    D. never be swept into the gutter

18._____

19. According to the rules and regulations of the department of parks, any violation of the rules and regulations

    A. is punishable by not more than 60 days imprisonment
    B. is punishable by a fine of not more than 100 dollars
    C. shall be deemed to be a misdemeanor unless otherwise so designated by the trial judge or the rules and regulations
    D. shall be triable by a city magistrate

19._____

20. According to the rules and regulations of the department of parks, possession in parks of merchandise in quantities, packages or containers customarily associated with peddling shall be deemed to be _____ evidence of offering for sale.

    A. circumstantial   B. conclusive
    C. presumptive   D. prima facie

20._____

21. According to the rules and regulations of the department of parks, unless duly licensed by the park commissioner, no person shall bring beer, ale or other alcoholic beverages into any park

    A. at any time
    B. except on legal holidays
    C. in containers having a capacity of more than a quart
    D. when the bottle, flask, or container thereof has been opened prior to entering upon park property

21._____

22. Select the one of the following which is untrue according to the rules and regulations of the department of parks:

    A. Instruction in operating automobiles or motorcycles is permitted in certain areas of parks and park-streets if a prior permit has been granted by the park commissioner
    B. Invalid wheelchairs may be pushed along a boardwalk or a pedestrian walk without a license from the park commissioner
    C. In no case is cruising by a taxi in a park permitted
    D. Persons may push bicycles in a single file in a park to a place in a park designated for riding such bicycles

23. Our public city playgrounds fall into five general classifications.
    Select the one of the following which is NOT one of these five classifications:

    A. Neighborhood   B. Marginal
    C. School   D. Shoestring

24. Parkway gasoline service stations differ from other concessions in the park department with respect to the manner in which such concessionaires are selected MAINLY because such parkway gasoline service station concessions are granted on the basis of

    A. potential ability to operate successfully
    B. competitive bidding
    C. demonstrated experience
    D. financial responsibility

25. When two men are carrying a long object such as a plank, the one of the following which is LEAST important from a safety standpoint is that the

    A. load should be put down at the same time by both men
    B. two men should be of the same height
    C. two men should be in step
    D. plank should be carried on the same shoulder, that is right or left, of each man

26. Injuries are frequently caused when a workman, in lifting a heavy object, bends his back rather than bending his knees and, at the same time, keeping his back straight. Such injuries USUALLY result from pressure on the

    A. arms and shoulders
    B. collar bone and upper vertebrae (spine)
    C. lower spine
    D. ribs

27. A ten-year analysis of the major causes of fire, conducted fairly recently by the National Board of Fire Under writers, showed that of the following, the one that caused the HIGHEST percentage of fires was

    A. matches and smoking
    B. misuse of electricity
    C. spontaneous combustion
    D. stoves, furnaces, and defective chimneys

28. In painting operations, the costs are generally about _____ labor, _____ paint.

    A. 50%; 50%   B. 60%; 40%   C. 70%; 30%   D. 80%; 20%

29. There are two distinct types of reel type lawn mowers–the *side wheel* drive and the *rear wheel* drive.
    The one of the following concerning these two types of mowers which is TRUE is that

    A. a side wheel mower is usually faster than the rear wheel mower
    B. on the side wheel mower, the wheels generally operate within the width of the cutting unit
    C. the side wheel mower generally permits closer trimming next to walls or obstructions than the rear wheel mower
    D. the side wheel mower usually has a narrower wheel base than the rear wheel mower

30. The fuel mixture in a high production professional chain saw is usually _____ gasoline and _____ oil.

    A. high octane; detergent
    B. high octane; non-detergent
    C. regular; detergent
    D. regular; non-detergent

31. A windrow deflector on a large power mower would be designed MAINLY to

    A. enable the machine to follow ground contours easily
    B. permit a very small turning radius
    C. prevent compaction of the turf
    D. scatter clippings uniformly

32. On a *Toro Professional Mower* with a 3 unit assembly, the one of the following which is CLOSEST to the operator's seat is the

    A. choke
    B. oil bath air cleaner
    C. reel clutch control
    D. roller bracket

33. Concerning the air cleaner on the *Whirlwind Model GK-Rotary-Scythe*, it would be MOST accurate to state that

    A. after it is cleaned, the air cleaner should be filled with fresh motor oil and gasoline
    B. the filter element should be soaked in gasoline
    C. it should be cleaned everytime the motor oil is changed
    D. the unit need not be dismantled in order to clean it

34. Concerning the motor lubrication of the ZIPPER 36" Sickle Bar Mower, it would be MOST accurate to state that the

    A. oil should be changed daily
    B. oil should be drained while motor is cool
    C. crankcase should be flushed when the oil is changed
    D. motor need not be stopped to check the oil level

35. In starting the motor of a *Gravely sickle and reel*, it would be MOST correct to state that

    A. before cranking motor the clutch levers should be in the middle position
    B. six or eight pulls on the starting strap are needed to start the motor
    C. the starting strap is wound counterclockwise around the lower fan pulley
    D. the throttle must be open all the way

36. If it is necessary to restore to its proper consistency white lead paint which has hardened due to cool weather, it is BEST to do this by   36.____

   A. the addition of boiled linseed oil
   B. the addition of turpentine
   C. vigorous stirring of the paint
   D. warming the paint

37. Bituminous surfaces often develop *map-cracked* surfaces which resemble boundary lines on maps.   37.____
   Such map-cracked areas on bituminous surfaces should be spot sealed

   A. any time of the year when the cracks are thoroughly dry
   B. only in the spring and during dry weather
   C. preferably in the summer and in rather warm weather
   D. any time of the year regardless of whether the cracks are wet or dry

38. According to generally accepted safety requirements and practices, the one of the following jobs that MUST be done under the supervision of the foreman of mechanics is   38.____

   A. applying boiler compound
   B. inspecting and recharging fire extinguishers
   C. lubricating unit heater motors
   D. lubricating vacuum pumps and motors

39. The knot that is USUALLY recommended for tying tools to be raised into a tree is a   39.____

   A. clove hitch   B. figure of eight
   C. sheet bend   D. square

40. The LARGEST individual item of expense in operating a public building is generally the cost of   40.____

   A. cleaning
   B. heating
   C. lighting
   D. repairing toilet plumbing

41. It is recommended that all tree-pruning wounds 3/4 inch or more in diameter be painted to protect the tree. The BEST paint to use, of the following, is   41.____

   A. a rubber base paint   B. an alkyd resin paint
   C. emulsified asphalt   D. red lead

42. With respect to lightning and trees, it would be MOST accurate to state that   42.____

   A. all species of trees appear to have the same susceptibility to attack by lightning
   B. lightning damage to tree root systems is rare
   C. the total damage done to a tree by a bolt of lightning is not always immediately apparent
   D. trees with shallow widespreading root systems are more liable to lightning injury than deep-rooted trees

43. An adequate supply of humus in the soil is one of the most important factors in a program of good soil management.
The one of the following statements about humus which is UNTRUE is that humus

   A. increases the water-holding capacity of soils
   B. modifies the soil structure
   C. readily absorbs the sun's rays
   D. retards the bacterial action in the soil to a very marked degree

44. The modern, widely available insect killers in common use fall MAINLY into three groups. The one of the following which is NOT one of these recognized groups is the

   A. botanicals
   B. chlorinated hydrocarbons
   C. cleaginous petroleums
   D. organic phosphates

45. Inorganic commercial fertilizers are the most common types used today. They are made in various mixtures. A 5-10-5 inorganic commercial fertilizer contains 5% _____, 10% _____, and 5% _____.

   A. nitrogen; phosphorous; potash
   B. nitrogen; potash; phosphorous
   C. nitrogen; potassium; potash
   D. phosphorous; nitrogen; potash

46. Against chewing insects such as caterpillars and beetles, it would be BEST to use a

   A. contact insecticide with a fine droplet mist or fog
   B. residual or surface insecticide in a coarser or wet spray
   C. space of knock-down insecticide in a coarser or wet spray
   D. space or knock-down insecticide with a fine droplet mist or fog

47. A hand-operated earth auger would be MOST likely used to

   A. cut weeds
   B. edge turf
   C. tamp sod
   D. test soil

48. In an inspection report, one of the items concerning a lawn area reads, *Fill in depression, grade, and embellish.* *Embellish* here means MOST NEARLY

   A. add fertilizer to
   B. improve the appearance of
   C. aerate
   D. roll

49. *Areas shall be scarified manually until the surface is friable.*
Friable in this sentence means MOST NEARLY

   A. easily crumbled into powder
   B. free of debris and organic matter
   C. free of rock
   D. raked evenly

50. To characterize a leaf as *serrated* means MOST NEARLY that the leaf

   A. is full of insects
   B. has an autumnal color
   C. has sawlike notches along the edge
   D. is semi-circular in shape

KEY (CORRECT ANSWERS)

1. B	11. C	21. C	31. D	41. C
2. B	12. B	22. A	32. C	42. C
3. A	13. D	23. D	33. C	43. D
4. B	14. C	24. B	34. A	44. C
5. C	15. C	25. B	35. A	45. A
6. D	16. B	26. C	36. D	46. B
7. C	17. C	27. A	37. D	47. D
8. D	18. B	28. D	38. A	48. B
9. A	19. D	29. A	39. A	49. A
10. D	20. D	30. D	40. A	50. C

EXAMINATION SECTION
TEST 1

DIRECTIONS: Each question or incomplete statement is followed by several suggested answers or completions. Select the one that BEST answers the question or completes the statement. *PRINT THE LETTER OF THE CORRECT ANSWER IN THE SPACE AT THE RIGHT.*

1. A well-conceived and effectively presented budget should do each of the following EXCEPT

    A. inform taxpayers and government officials of the amounts of money spent, the sources of revenue, and the costs of achieving departmental goals
    B. serve for evaluating the program and ensuring that objectives are met
    C. help in promoting flexible operational procedures by creating very few classifications for all expenditures, and requiring flexible procedures for approving them
    D. provide a general statement of the financial needs, resources, and plans of the department, including an outline of all program elements and their costs and allocations for facilities and personnel

2. Among volunteers who offer time to park and recreation departments, which of the following motivating factors is most prevalent?

    A. Preparation for paid employment
    B. Family influences
    C. A desire to feel needed
    D. A desire to be helpful

3. Which of the following approaches to leisure service is found chiefly among recreation and park managers who serve in resource-based agencies?

    A. Individualist
    B. Prescriptive
    C. Environmental/aesthetic
    D. Human-services

4. In most public park and recreation departments, the largest area of use for volunteer workers is in

    A. direct leadership of groups or assisting professional leaders at work
    B. specialized educational appointments
    C. clerical assistance and helping with mailings, reports, and similar assignments
    D. administrative, promotional, or advisory activities

5. The use of night lighting at outdoor recreational facilities typically creates each of the following benefits EXCEPT

    A. deterring personal crime
    B. overall lower cost per hour of public use
    C. beautification of the park by enhancing plants, trees, and architectural features
    D. distinguishing activities within the park

6. Of the four types of in-service training administered to entry-level park and recreation employees, which is most likely to be delivered on an individual basis?

A. General career development
B. Training to keep the worker up to date
C. Orientation to the job
D. Training related specifically to the position for which the employee was selected

7. In recent years, community leisure-service organizations have adopted each of the following methods for achieving a high degree of productivity and efficiency EXCEPT

    A. cost-cutting practices
    B. zero-based budgeting
    C. a more extensive use of cost-benefit analysis
    D. reduced contracting, concession, and leasing arrangements

8. Which of the following statements concerning contributory negligence and children is TRUE?
    A child
    I. under 7 years of age is conclusively adjudged to be incapable of contributory negligence
    II. between 7 and 10 years of age is rebuttably presumed to be incapable of negligence
    III. over fourteen years of age is presumed capable of negligence
    The CORRECT answer is:

    A. I only   B. I, II   C. I, III   D. II, III

9. In general, a daily program schedule is divided into blocks of time, with major blocks of time of an hour or more per block incorporated. Generally, the daily program schedule is arranged with

    A. one block of time scheduled in the morning and one in the afternoon
    B. one in the morning and two in the afternoon
    C. only one major block per day, usually in the morning
    D. only one major block per day, usually in the afternoon

10. The MAIN advantage of an unstructured, decentralized approach to recreational programming is

    A. being able to respond to local neighborhood needs and special characteristics
    B. a set of core activities that meet clear program guidelines
    C. more intimate contact between community members and recreational leaders
    D. more efficient use of personnel resources

11. According to the Management-by-Objectives model (MBO), which of the following is NOT a guideline for the setting of park and recreation agency objectives?

    A. Objectives must be broad and open to interpretation by evaluators.
    B. Personnel at each level should play a role in setting their own objectives.
    C. A limited number of major objectives should be used for each unit or individual.
    D. Each objective should be given a precise time limit for accomplishment.

12. Which of the following steps in the purchasing process of a public agency would typically occur FIRST?   12.____

    A. Justification   B. Bids
    C. Specifications   D. Purchase orders

13. Of the various types of fees and charges at their disposal, public recreation and park departments most often use   13.____

    A. entrance/admission fees   B. lease revenue
    C. program/activity fees   D. rental fees

14. When a park and recreation official has the opportunity to speak with the media about the operations of the department, he or she should   14.____

    A. speak in 30-second quotes, or shorter
    B. use technical language that will show the significance of the project or organization
    C. dress in bright colors
    D. use preface remarks

15. Each of the following is an advantage associated with contracting out various functions of a public park and recreation department EXCEPT   15.____

    A. greater departmental independence
    B. avoiding the restrictions of bureaucratic structures and similar political institutions
    C. lower personnel costs
    D. clearer contractual specification of quantity, quality, and price of work

16. Which of the following is NOT a growing trend in the personnel assignment policies of larger park and recreation departments?   16.____

    A. Having a fixed number of full-time, year-round employees supplemented by a limited number of specialists during the year, and an influx of summer workers for playground or camping programs
    B. Greater responsibility of *face-to-face* leaders in coordinating and directing programs
    C. Assignment of leaders to other district- or city-wide roles which can be carried out during slack periods
    D. Rotation of assignments at different seasons

17. According to most current practices in public agencies, the first work sessions on the departmental budget for the following year are generally held in the months of   17.____

    A. March-April   B. May-June
    C. August-September   D. October-November

18. Which of the following appears to have the LEAST significant effect on a person's opportunities to engage in recreational activities?   18.____

    A. Time
    B. Geographic and environmental resources
    C. Motivation
    D. Health and fitness

19. A park and recreation department's _____ is a document that includes planned and proposed expenditures for carrying out major purchases and construction projects of a substantial and long-term nature.

    A. operating budget
    B. balance sheet
    C. capital budget
    D. performance budget

20. A large park of several hundred acres will generally provide _____ acres of area for every user.

    A. 1-2   B. 5   C. 10   D. 20

21. Concerning intramural and extramural sports programs, most park and recreation departments have specific policies designed to deal with the issue of forfeited contests. Which of the following is NOT generally one of these policies?

    A. A team or individual not ready to play within thirty minutes after the scheduled time is charged with a forfeit.
    B. An individual or team may be assessed a forfeit fee.
    C. Two forfeits result in the elimination of an individual or team from all further participation in that sport.
    D. If a team or individual leaves before the forfeit is duly noted by an official or supervisor, then both teams should be charged with a forfeit.

22. Most local park and recreation agencies function within a framework of legislation provided by the

    A. federal government
    B. state government
    C. municipal government
    D. appointed board

23. Within a working group assigned to a specific task, the task structure is measured by each of the following EXCEPT the degree to which

    A. members understand what the goal is
    B. the correctness of a decision can be demonstrated by authority or logic
    C. multiple paths to the goal are evident
    D. one solution is more correct

24. During a summer recreation program, quiet activities are usually BEST scheduled for

    A. as late in the day as possible
    B. the early afternoon
    C. mid-day
    D. the early morning

25. Which of the following statements about adolescent recreationists is FALSE?

    A. They generally show a rapid increase in lung capacity.
    B. They are capable not only of describing, but of explaining situations or phenomena.
    C. Norms for male or female behavior are generally discovered through interactions with the opposite sex.
    D. They are concerned with the meaning of life according to religious and philosophical perspectives.

KEY (CORRECT ANSWERS)

1.	C	11.	A
2.	D	12.	A
3.	C	13.	C
4.	A	14.	A
5.	B	15.	A
6.	C	16.	A
7.	D	17.	B
8.	C	18.	C
9.	B	19.	C
10.	A	20.	B

21. A
22. B
23. C
24. C
25. C

TEST 2

DIRECTIONS: Each question or incomplete statement is followed by several suggested answers or completions. Select the one that BEST answers the question or completes the statement. *PRINT THE LETTER OF THE CORRECT ANSWER IN THE SPACE AT THE RIGHT.*

1. In developing any recreation program, an administrator's primary emphasis is nearly always on

    A. education for leisure
    B. providing organized or supervised activities
    C. coordinating and assisting functions
    D. providing facilities for unscheduled and unsupervised use

2. Each of the following is a disadvantage associated with the use of air-supported structures as a housing for recreational facilities EXCEPT

    A. their susceptibility to vandalism
    B. their short life expectancy
    C. lack of flexibility in yearly program scheduling
    D. possible zoning law conflicts

3. Typically, which of the following would be the final step in the development of a maintenance management plan for a recreational facility?
The

    A. definition of the maintenance plan's overall goals and objectives
    B. development of work order request forms for non-routine, nonrecurring maintenance tasks
    C. creation of a format for scheduling maintenance work
    D. development of a form for daily maintenance work and assignments

4. In liability terms, each of the following is a means of risk reduction for a park and recreation department EXCEPT

    A. conducting periodic safety inspections for all facilities and equipment
    B. training all employees in safety practices, first aid, and preventive maintenance
    C. clearly labeling potential risks to users
    D. developing safety rules for the operation of facilities and equipment

5. Managing a public park and recreation department like a business, using marketing strategies, has proven effective for many departments in trimming costs and streamlining services, but the marketing approach does have several disadvantages. Which of the following is NOT generally considered to be one of them?

    A. The bottom line of program development is profitability.
    B. Efforts at securing public subsidies are likely to be reduced.
    C. Services to poorer community residents may atrophy.
    D. Possible ventures may be evaluated only in terms of who will be able to pay for them.

6. The need for public relations in the field of parks and recreation is enforced by certain prevailing public attitudes. Which of the following is NOT generally considered to be one of these prevailing attitudes?

    A. Frequent occasions, brought about by the very nature of park and recreation operations, when individual citizens become irritated, frustrated, or disappointed
    B. Limited knowledge of the range of services and programs offered
    C. A generalized opposition to public funding of a department that is not considered to be part of the infrastructure
    D. The feeling that public recreation is not really a necessity; that the public is able to meet its leisure needs independently

7. In most states, the statute of limitations for litigating actions involving negligence is

    A. 1 year
    B. 2 years
    C. 10 years
    D. in most states, there is no statute of limitations

8. In park and recreation management applications, a *diagraph* is used to

    A. view the community-wide availability of programs and detect under- or over-provision of different types of activities on a geographical basis
    B. show all events or continuing activities in a convenient and easily understood form
    C. show individual projects or programs laid out along a calendar, with specific tasks indicated for the dates on which they are to be begun and completed
    D. identify major facilities and ongoing programs

9. Which of the following is considered to be the responsibility of a program-administrative staff member at a park and recreation department?

    A. Monitoring personnel practices
    B. Preparing statistical or analytical reports of operations
    C. Monitoring facility use and operations
    D. Implementing policies for safety

10. The probationary period for most newly-hired park and recreation personnel is

    A. 24-48 hours   B. 4-6 weeks
    C. 3-6 months   D. 1-2 years

11. For busy community members who have fluctuating schedules, and who want to compete in a more structured competitive environment, a recreation and park department's most effective way of dealing with competitive sports such as tennis is to establish a _____ tournament structure for participants.

    A. single elimination   B. double elimination
    C. challenge   D. round-robin

12. A specific tax leveled against the assessed value of residential or industrial property, the amount of which is assigned directly to the public park and recreation fund and used exclusively for that purpose, is known as a(n) _____ tax.

    A. millage   B. real estate
    C. impact   D. levy

13. A _____ approach to leisure service sees recreation not as an activity carried on for its own sake, but as designed to accomplish specific therapeutic goals.

    A. human-services
    B. marketing
    C. individualist
    D. prescriptive

14. Which of the following steps in the development of a park and recreation program is typically administered first?

    A. Establishing goals, objectives, and policies
    B. Identifying the range of possible activities and services
    C. Assessing participant or community needs and interests
    D. Developing a program plan

15. The growing trend in park and recreation departmental budgeting is toward the use of _____ budgets.

    A. program
    B. function classification
    C. performance
    D. line-item

16. What type of accounting system shows, on updated expenditure reports, all encumbrances or charges against specified accounts?

    A. Balance sheet
    B. Concurrent auditing
    C. Work program auditing
    D. Accrual

17. Which of the following statements about recreationists in middle childhood (6-12 years) is generally TRUE?

    A. Their muscles develop in function, but are still immature in size and strength.
    B. They have not mastered the concept of numbers, clock time, or calendar time.
    C. They do not exhibit abstract thought processes.
    D. They know rules which specify right from wrong, but may not understand the reasoning behind them.

18. Which of the following is NOT a typical benefit associated with informal structures and processes within the framework of a park and recreation department?

    A. Enhancement of a manager's authority
    B. Reduced time requirements for developing projects
    C. Increased opportunity for lower-level personnel to share meaningfully in agency planning
    D. Improved planning and problem-solving functions

19. Which of the following administration philosophies or strategies is NOT part of the future-oriented trend in park and recreation management?

    A. Evaluating services in terms of human consequences
    B. Offering programs anywhere in the community, with staff resources helping residents develop their own leadership skills
    C. Funding all basic programs from tax allocations
    D. Acting in an enabling or catalyzing role in matching community resources to citizen's needs

20. When a recreation and park manager has news of interest to the local newspaper, there are several approaches he or she might take. Which of the following should be used most sparingly?

    A. Arranging a news conference and invite interested reporters and editors
    B. Calling the newspaper, summarizing the information briefly to the appropriate editor or reporter, and allowing the person to suggest a course of action
    C. Writing the information in the form of a *letter to the editor* and mail or deliver it to the editor
    D. Preparing a news release and mail or deliver it to the editor

21. Each of the following is a typical policy used by park and recreation departments concerning the reservation of recreational facilities by community members EXCEPT

    A. cancellations must be made in person with the proper identification
    B. cancellations must be made 24 hours in advance, or a no-show penalty will apply
    C. persons absent 10 minutes past the reserved time forfeit all rights to the facility
    D. reservations must be made at least 4 hours in advance

22. In a departmental budget, the function of a work program is *primarily* to

    A. determine scheduling needs for the coming year
    B. estimate personnel expenditures
    C. establish a clear set of administrative performance standards
    D. outline tasks to be performed, standards of service and efficiency, and methods to be used

23. While conducting a needs assessment of the community, park and recreation administrators relate the leisure services currently offered to a set of national standards for such services in similar communities. In this situation, the administration is determining the community's _____ need for services.

    A. expressed   B. normative
    C. perceived   D. relative

24. Which of the following is not typically a heading used on a written maintenance plan for a recreational facility?

    A. Personnel   B. Chain of command
    C. Maintenance standards   D. Frequency

25. According to the established national standard, a park and recreation manager who is planning a leisure facility should rely upon the figure of 1 acre of land needed for every _____ community residents.

    A. 100   B. 800   C. 1200   D. 2500

KEY (CORRECT ANSWERS)

1. D
2. C
3. B
4. C
5. B

6. C
7. B
8. B
9. A
10. C

11. C
12. A
13. D
14. C
15. A

16. D
17. D
18. A
19. C
20. A

21. D
22. D
23. B
24. B
25. B

EXAMINATION SECTION
TEST 1

DIRECTIONS: Each question or incomplete statement is followed by several suggested answers or completions. Select the one that BEST answers the question or completes the statement. *PRINT THE LETTER OF THE CORRECT ANSWER IN THE SPACE AT THE RIGHT.*

1. For a large public park and recreation department, it is generally agreed that the key to productivity is

    A. contracting and leasing arrangements
    B. the effective management of personnel
    C. cost-benefit analysis
    D. appealing to private foundations for funds

    1._____

2. In a park and recreation setting, four conditions must be present in a situation in order for the department to be found legally negligent, and therefore liable, in the case of an accident. Which of the following is NOT one of these conditions?

    A. Proof of injury or damage
    B. Legal responsibility for the participant
    C. The participant's lack of an employment relationship to the department
    D. The department's failure to take reasonable care

    2._____

3. In a park and recreation department, the MOST effective approach to problem-solving is generally described as

    A. group-centered
    B. authoritarian
    C. decisions by higher authorities
    D. an analysis by planning specialists

    3._____

4. Which of the following administration philosophies or strategies is part of the future-oriented trend in park and recreation management?

    A. Planning programs with the staff, chiefly by updating past programs
    B. Evaluating outcomes primarily through attendance figures
    C. Providing programs and services based on social and economic needs of the community
    D. Requiring financial accountability and justifying budgets based on historical precedent

    4._____

5. The _____ approach to leisure service sees recreation as an important community service that is carried on both for its own sake and because it contributes to the mental and physical health of participants.

    A. human-services   B. prescriptive
    C. environmental   D. quality-of-life

    5._____

6. More or increased _____ is NOT a growing trend in leisure services.

    A. centralized personnel structure
    B. emphasis on health and fitness

    6._____

C. consideration of leisure's contribution to quality of life
D. emphasis on noncompetitive forms of play

7. The MOST common means of financing public recreation and park departments is through

   A. bonds
   B. grants
   C. taxes
   D. fees and charges

8. For evaluating the effectiveness of specific programs offered by a park and recreation department, each of the following methods is commonly used EXCEPT

   A. systems-based, goal-achievement models
   B. internal auditing by top management
   C. staff-based evaluation processes
   D. participant-based evaluation

9. A public agency that favors the delegation of authority is BEST described as

   A. heterogeneous
   B. decentralized
   C. individualistic
   D. irresponsible

10. The ability to _____ is NOT generally considered to be a core process that an entry-level employee in a park and recreation department should master.

    A. carry out both program planning and organizational planning
    B. formally articulate resource needs
    C. utilize leadership processes
    D. teach

11. A _____ budget is designed in such a way that large units of work, or special programs, are isolated, identified, and described in detail.

    A. object classification
    B. function classification
    C. program
    D. performance

12. When programming recreational activities for participants in middle childhood (6-12 years), it is important to remember that they are generally

    A. preferring separation into sexually segregated groups
    B. physically aggressive
    C. physically growing more quickly than in preschool years
    D. unconcerned about ideas such as competence, achievement, and approval from others

13. Of the following issues, _____ is LEAST likely to be negotiated in a park and recreation labor union contractual agreement.

    A. work hours
    B. contracting work, or *outsourcing*
    C. safety regulations
    D. retirement plans

14. Which of the following is considered to be the responsibility of an auxiliary staff member at a park and recreation department?

    A. Supervision of sport programs
    B. Monitoring adherence to agency rules
    C. Direction of administrative guidelines
    D. Organizing sport activities

15. Traditionally, leisure facilities have been planned according to

    A. concepts of the neighborhood and community
    B. urban planning methods based on land-use principles
    C. a needs index
    D. recommended standards of open space

16. Public agencies such as park and recreation departments typically use one of several contemporary models in evaluating whether the agency has achieved its stated objectives. Which of the following is NOT one of these models?
    Evaluation designed to measure the

    A. overall quality of programs, based on the opinion of an advisory board
    B. effectiveness of programs in meeting their stated goals and objectives
    C. effectiveness of personnel in carrying out stated program goals and objectives
    D. level of satisfaction of program participants

17. It is NOT typically a function of a public park and recreation agency's board or commission to

    A. review and approve all policies and work with the agency's managers to develop plans for meeting present and future leisure needs of the community
    B. consider and approve all personnel appointments or promotions
    C. articulate to the agency's director and staff how the details of administration should be carried out
    D. carry out long-range planning in cooperation with other community organizations to meet public recreational needs

18. In handling employment inquiries, application forms, and interviews for employment, questions to the applicant about _____ may be allowed under law, whether their use is job-related or not.

    A. employment history
    B. physical requirements
    C. arrest and conviction record
    D. age

19. According to most current practices in public agencies, any overspending or underspending in the year's budget is to be brought to the department head's attention in the month of

    A. January
    B. February
    C. March or April
    D. November

20. In order to avoid legal liability for certain activities involving children, some park and recreation departments use the convention of permission slips signed by a parent or guardian, in which they are asked to waive the right to sue in case of injury or accident. For several reasons, these slips offer the department a false sense of security. Which of the following is NOT one of these reasons?
    I. In all cases, signed statements are invalid if the risks of the activity are not understood.
    II. The waiver is not valid unless signed by both parents, no matter what their geographic location.
    III. They cannot waive the right of a child to bring suit against the agency when the child reaches the legal age for doing so.

    The CORRECT answer is:

    A. I only   B. I, II   C. I, III   D. I, II, III

21. Which of the following recreation facilities would most likely be located at or near the intersection of major or secondary thoroughfares near the center of a 4- or 5-square mile service area?

    A. Playlot
    B. Large park
    C. Playground
    D. Athletic field

22. Which of the following is NOT a level of planning commonly associated with recreation and park facilities?

    A. Planning that focuses solely on recreation and park development within a total community, sometimes as a separate portion of a total plan
    B. Regional planning that takes into account services and facilities offered by adjacent jurisdictions
    C. Planning that is concerned with the development of a particular facility or the needs of a single neighborhood
    D. Total master planning that considers all aspects of municipal growth, including industrial and residential development, transportation, education, housing, health, etc.

23. The MAIN advantage of a structured, centralized approach to recreational programming is

    A. being able to respond to local neighborhood needs
    B. optimum legal protection from liability claims
    C. more efficient use of personnel resources
    D. a set of clear-cut standards for fulfilling the agency's stated objectives

24. When programming recreational activities for participants in middle adulthood (40-65 years), it is important to remember that they generally

    A. experience physiological changes in the brain
    B. begin to experience instability in cognitive skills
    C. display a loss of creativity
    D. tend to gain weight easily

25. In park and recreation accounting, concurrent auditing represents 25.____
    A. a preaudit of expected income or disbursements
    B. a formal check of specific administrative or program divisions of a department, or construction or maintenance projects
    C. a form of bookkeeping report showing the assets and liabilities of a given fund or budget
    D. all departmental expenditures that have been authorized and carried out

KEY (CORRECT ANSWERS)

1.	B	11.	C
2.	C	12.	A
3.	A	13.	B
4.	C	14.	A
5.	D	15.	C
6.	A	16.	A
7.	C	17.	C
8.	B	18.	A
9.	B	19.	B
10.	B	20.	C

21. D
22. B
23. D
24. D
25. A

TEST 2

DIRECTIONS: Each question or incomplete statement is followed by several suggested answers or completions. Select the one that BEST answers the question or completes the statement. *PRINT THE LETTER OF THE CORRECT ANSWER IN THE SPACE AT THE RIGHT.*

1. Each of the following is a benefit associated with the use of a *matrix* structure in a public park and recreation department EXCEPT

    A. greater opportunity of employees' personal development
    B. better technical performance
    C. improved flexibility in conditions of change and uncertainty
    D. involvement in long-range planning of employees at every level

2. Which of the following statements about recreationists in early adulthood (20-39 years) is generally TRUE?

    A. They are more self-centered than adolescents.
    B. Their friendships are characterized by less intimacy.
    C. They experience a lack of stability in intellectual skills.
    D. They expand their social relationships through new contacts within the occupational and community settings.

3. When programming recreation activities, an administrator's choices are likely to be affected by each of the following factors EXCEPT

    A. the number of potential activities
    B. the characteristics of participants
    C. the funds required
    D. personnel

4. A recreation programmer wants to stage a single-elimination summer softball tournament at the department's facilities. Each of the following is an advantage associated with the single-elimination format EXCEPT it

    A. is usually more interesting for spectators
    B. may accommodate a large number of participants
    C. encourages maximum participation
    D. is the most economical to conduct

5. In a recreation or park facility's off-season, an administrator wants to maintain a minimum level of care. Typically, how often should litter at the facility be picked up?

    A. Daily
    C. Monthly
    B. Weekly
    D. Every two months

6. Funding agencies for public park and recreation departments have historically applied strict criteria for determining grant recipients. Which of the following statements about their considerations is generally FALSE?

    A. There must be evidence that existing programs and facilities are being fully utilized.
    B. Agencies applying for grants must be prepared to guarantee a substantial portion of the total grant proposal.

C. Higher priority is given to proposals that come from more than one agency or sponsor.
D. Wherever possible, grant proposals should be designed to serve the general population, rather than isolated or special-need communities.

7. In public recreation programs, sport accounts for about _____% of all active involvement.

   A. 10-30 B. 35-50 C. 60-75 D. 80-95

8. Which of the following is NOT a level of responsibility defined by the functional classification of personnel analysis?

   A. Managerial
   B. Tutorial
   C. Logistical
   D. Operational

9. During a community needs assessment, a park and recreation department would most likely conduct use surveys among the community members in order to determine the _____ leisure needs of the community.

   A. expressed B. normative C. relative D. perceived

10. The main disadvantage to using an *object classification* type of budget for a park and recreation department is that

    A. it does not relate expenditures meaningfully to programs
    B. certain expenditures, such as personnel, are not considered *objects*
    C. it does not provide complete itemization of expenditures
    D. it does not take unplanned expenditures into account

11. Which of the following is NOT a guideline to follow in preparing a newspaper release for a public park and recreation department event or service?

    A. The release should stick to the facts and avoid editorializing.
    B. An attempt should be made to feature a prominent or interesting individual or group of people in the article.
    C. The most important information should be included at the beginning of the article.
    D. The release should be limited to 2 or 3 pages.

12. In a public school or college's recreational facilities, the priority of use must be

    A. intramural or campus recreational programming
    B. intercollegiate practice sessions or competition
    C. formal academic program use
    D. community residents

13. For a supervisor in a park and recreation department, each of the following is a guideline to follow in taking disciplinary action with employees EXCEPT

    A. when correction is required, it should be handled in private
    B. the worker should be told what he or she can do to correct the situation
    C. the action should not be taken until some time after the need for it has been established
    D. take the same corrective actions for the same behaviors with different individuals

14. The healthiest way a park and recreation department manager can approach the subject of inter-employee conflict is to view it as

    A. inevitable, but desirable and able to be used to constructive ends
    B. a healthy sign that workers in the department intend to challenge and compete with one another to meet departmental goals
    C. an inevitable product of a close working relationship that should be not denied, but endured peaceably
    D. a harmful and destructive influence that should be avoided at all costs

15. Which of the following is NOT generally considered to be a guideline to follow in determining when, and for what, recreation fees and charges are justified?

    A. Frequently charge where *preservation* is the dominant function
    B. Be sure that some benefit accrues to the taxpayer
    C. The specific services to be charged for and the fee should be matters of local choice
    D. Frequently charge where *use* is the dominant function

16. Generally, which of the following approaches to urban planning is used LEAST often?

    A. Developing an ideal model of the community
    B. Cost-revenue model
    C. User-oriented approach
    D. Needs index model

17. When conditions within a working group are only moderately favorable or unfavorable (i.e., the leader is well-liked but the task under consideration is unstructured), what type of leadership style is most appropriate?

    A. Laissez-faire   B. Task-oriented
    C. Authoritarian   D. Relationship-oriented

18. In a park and recreation department, a cost-benefit analysis is LEAST likely to be useful for

    A. identifying high- and low-cost programs and services as related to maintenance, administration, and direct leadership costs per participant-hour of service rendered
    B. providing valuable support data for justifying budget requests
    C. providing essential data for determining the cost-effectiveness of individual department personnel
    D. permitting the assignment of priorities to specific programs and services

19. In recent years, the number of volunteers working for public park and recreation departments has increased among certain segments of the population. Among the following groups, which has shown the LEAST significant increase in volunteer service?

    A. Females   B. Males
    C. Poor people   D. Minorities

20. The major type of legislation affecting parks and recreation is the

    A. regulatory law   B. special district law
    C. enabling law   D. home rule legislation

21. When programming recreational activities for participants in late adulthood (over 65 years), it is important to remember that they generally

 A. do not require a significant restructuring of time
 B. have a self-concept that tends to be more dependent upon external factors
 C. prefer to live in close contact with others of their age group
 D. become less active if they are men, and more active if they are women

22. The self-study approach to agency evaluation, outlined by the National Recreation and Park Association, includes standards that are used in measuring the effectiveness of a department in several major categories. Which of the following is NOT one of these categories?

 A. Administration B. Evaluation
 C. Programming D. Funding

23. Decisions made at the lower level of an agency's management, which are part of operational planning and program implementation, are described as _____ decisions.

 A. primary B. problem-oriented
 C. reflex D. task-oriented

24. In park and recreation applications, a *flowchart* is used to

 A. view the community-wide availability of programs and detect under- or over-provision of different types of activities on a geographical basis
 B. show all events or continuing activities in a convenient and easily understood form
 C. show individual projects or programs laid out along a calendar, with specific tasks indicated for the dates on which they are to be begun and completed
 D. identify major facilities and ongoing programs

25. In recreation and sports injury cases involving parents and children, the parents, but not the child, can be barred from recovery for a child's injury under certain conditions. Which of the following is NOT one of these conditions?
 The

 A. parent has failed to exercise reasonable care to prevent the child from placing himself in a situation in which lack of self-protective capacity may reasonably be expected to result in harm to the child
 B. child is too young to exercise self-protection
 C. child's incapacity is a contributing factor in harm
 D. injury involves an *attractive nuisance*

KEY (CORRECT ANSWERS)

1.	D	11.	D
2.	D	12.	C
3.	A	13.	C
4.	C	14.	A
5.	A	15.	A
6.	D	16.	B
7.	C	17.	D
8.	B	18.	C
9.	D	19.	A
10.	A	20.	C

21. D
22. D
23. D
24. C
25. D

EXAMINATION SECTION
TEST 1

DIRECTIONS: Each question or incomplete statement is followed by several suggested answers or completions. Select the one that BEST answers the question or completes the statement. *PRINT THE LETTER OF THE CORRECT ANSWER IN THE SPACE AT THE RIGHT.*

1. The _____ goals of a park and recreation department consist of those outcomes the agency seeks to achieve by offering programs. 1.____

    A. external
    B. adaptation
    C. positional
    D. management

2. Most recreation professionals would include each of the following in a definition of *recreation* EXCEPT 2.____

    A. requiring personal and free choice on the part of the recreationist
    B. requiring a commitment by the recreationist
    C. rewarding insofar as the recreationist can establish and meet certain specific goals
    D. occurring during nonobligated time

3. For what type of bond is a *sinkable* fund generally used? 3.____

    A. Callable
    B. Serial
    C. Assessment
    D. Term

4. Which of the following would be involved in an assessment of a manager's socioemotional skills? 4.____

    A. Efficiency orientation
    B. Self-control
    C. Conceptualization
    D. Logical thought

5. Which of the following is NOT a typical guideline to be used in community recreation programming? 5.____

    A. Community recreation should meet significant social needs.
    B. Special groups in the community, such as the mentally or physically disabled, should be served by recreation programs that meet their social, emotional, creative, and physical needs.
    C. Recreational activities should involve fixed schedules, locations, and personnel that community members will be able to rely upon and schedule around with few surprises.
    D. Community recreation programs should be meaningfully interpreted to the public at large through effective public relations media and community relations activities.

6. The maintenance department of a park and recreation agency should maintain a workload file containing all copies of submitted forms. Which of the following is NOT a convincing reason for this? 6.____

    A. Workers often forget their assignments.
    B. The completed tasks reveal a dollar value useful during budgeting.

C. Originals may get lost.
D. A special request for priority consideration be made if delays jeopardize safety or morale.

7. As part of an overall effort to reduce costs, park and recreation departments are likely to decrease expenditures related to budget items such as each of the following EXCEPT

   A. gasoline consumption and number of vehicles in department pools
   B. purchase of consumable supplies (paper, paint, crayons, basketballs, etc.) that are dispensed to the public without fee or accountability
   C. special programs that are seasonal or infrequently scheduled
   D. subscriptions, memberships, and purchase of books and training films

8. The National Recreation and Park Association recommends that if a public swimming pool is built for a community, it provide _____ square feet of swimming area of every 1% to 3% of the community population.

   A. 5   B. 15   C. 25   D. 40

9. According to surveys of park and recreation employees at the non-managerial level, the MOST important motivating factor for working in the field is

   A. being part of a team and not letting them down
   B. good working conditions
   C. doing work that is perceived by the employee to be important and worthwhile
   D. appreciation by supervisors for work performed

10. In programming recreational sports contests or tournaments, a department sometimes declines to take complete responsibility for scheduling, and relies instead on a system of *instant* scheduling. Each of the following is an advantage associated with this system EXCEPT

    A. it encourages entries well before the final deadline
    B. participants do not need to be contacted until playoff time, unless there is a schedule change
    C. there is no need for a large physical setting to conduct the process for large numbers of people
    D. selection of alternate playing times is done by participants

11. The _____ budget represents a combination of the object and function classification methods.

    A. performance
    B. classification by fund
    C. classification by organizational units
    D. operating

12. In budget planning sessions, a diagraph can be used to provide information about each of the following EXCEPT

    A. areas of needed program service
    B. months of greatest and least congestion
    C. geographical relations between major facilities
    D. conflicts among special events

13. A summer camp program includes rigidly planned meals, a rising hour, and bedtime, but other phases of the program are planned by both counselors and campers. This program could best be described as

    A. totally nonstructured
    B. having a skeletal structure
    C. semistructured
    D. fully structured

    13.____

14. Typically, policymaking in public agencies is determined by each of the following EXCEPT

    A. departmental factors
    B. recommendations of professional societies
    C. recommendations of clientele
    D. professional literature

    14.____

15. Which of the following is considered to be the responsibility of a program staff member at a park and recreation department?

    A. Attending to equipment
    B. Supervising a playground
    C. Monitoring the operating budget
    D. Helping plan policies and procedures

    15.____

16. It is generally NOT a purpose of a public park and recreation department's public relations efforts to

    A. attempt to coordinate the actions and attitudes of the public and the organization that seeks to serve it
    B. disseminate information to the public
    C. alter the public's beliefs and actions through persuasion
    D. parry the negative efforts of political foes within the municipality or region

    16.____

17. In deciding whether or not to engage in a certain recreational activity, which of the following steps would a person typically assess FIRST?

    A. His or her own personal suitability to the activity
    B. The probability that participation actually will result in possible benefits
    C. The relative value of the activity
    D. The feasibility of participating

    17.____

18. A public park and recreation agency's most commonly exercised method of acquiring property for facilities is to

    A. secure an easement
    B. transfer lands or exchange properties from one government department to another
    C. compel subdividers into setting aside property for recreational and park use
    D. purchase the property directly from its owner

    18.____

19. In most litigation involving park and recreation departments, which of the following is LEAST likely to be the target of litigious action?

    A. The program sponsor
    B. Administrators or supervisors
    C. The employee whose conduct is a direct or proximate cause of the injury
    D. A volunteer serving as an administrative adviser

20. After recreation programs have been initially planned and presented, each of the following concepts will be useful to consider in making program modifications EXCEPT

    A. required facilities
    B. program life cycle
    C. methods of program presentation
    D. program structure and degree of centralization

21. With which of the following statements, about the unionization of park and recreation workers, would an agency head most likely DISAGREE? It has

    A. improved the welfare of the employees by gaining for them higher salaries and benefits than they would have otherwise received
    B. enhanced the organization's ability to offer programs and services on the days and at the times when they are most desired by the public
    C. enhanced management's ability to hire well-qualified personnel
    D. forced the organization to reduce the quantity of services it provides for the public

22. Which of the following is NOT likely to be included in the land records of a park and recreation department?

    A. Where the official deeds are filed
    B. Official actions affecting the title such as street vacations, etc.
    C. Non-liability insurance records
    D. Legal description of the land

23. A manager responds to an employee's grievance by saying he feels sorry for the employee, but cannot do anything to change the situation. The manager has offered a(n) _____ response.

    A. situational   B. sympathetic
    C. judgmental   D. empathetic

24. In a working environment involving a mature group, the leader defines what is to be done, but engages also in supporting behavior intended to contribute to the group's willingness to work at a task. According to situational leadership theory, this mode of leadership is called

    A. participating   B. telling
    C. selling   D. delegating

25. For a large organization such as a park and recreation department, the MOST important aspect of maintaining financial controls is/are
    A. keeping adequate financial records and preparing and submitting monthly reports relating expenditures to categories in the annual budget
    B. establishing and enforcing strict cost control procedures
    C. the department's procedures for purchasing supplies or equipment
    D. the department's procedural requirements for making and enforcing contractual agreements

KEY (CORRECT ANSWERS)

1.	A	11.	A
2.	C	12.	C
3.	D	13.	B
4.	B	14.	C
5.	C	15.	C
6.	A	16.	D
7.	C	17.	C
8.	B	18.	D
9.	C	19.	D
10.	C	20.	A

21. B
22. C
23. B
24. C
25. A

TEST 2

DIRECTIONS: Each question or incomplete statement is followed by several suggested answers or completions. Select the one that BEST answers the question or completes the statement. *PRINT THE LETTER OF THE CORRECT ANSWER IN THE SPACE AT THE RIGHT.*

1. Each of the following is a type of supervisory board or commission associated with public recreation and park departments EXCEPT 1.____

    A. semi-independent bodies with the power to make policy, but dependent on a higher governmental body that provides funding and to which they must report
    B. advisory boards or commissions with limited powers
    C. completely independent bodies with full authority for establishing and overseeing policy
    D. independent bodies which do not make policy, but are primarily responsible for locating and distributing funds associated with policies formulated by another body

2. Which of the following is NOT a key managerial function in the process of organizing? 2.____

    A. Determination of recruitment and hiring policies
    B. Defining goals and objectives
    C. Clustering functions within the organization
    D. Assigning responsibility to individuals and granting authority

3. The authority for raising taxes and spending money for municipal recreation services comes from 3.____

    A. state legislatures
    B. the local board
    C. local elections
    D. the welfare clauses of the Constitution

4. Studies in public parks and recreation departments have shown that although the public shows initial resistance to the imposition of new or increased fees for use of programs, services, and facilities, the short-term decline in usage tends to disappear within 4.____

    A. 6-8 months   B. 12-18 months
    C. 2-3 years   D. 3-5 years

5. For legal purposes, the standard of care owed to a user by a park and recreation department is determined by classifying the types of users into three broad categories. Which of the following is NOT one of these categories? 5.____

    A. Licensee   B. Trespasser
    C. Invitee   D. Grantee

6. The primary *disadvantage* associated with the use of a double-elimination format for scheduled recreational tournaments is that 6.____

    A. it does not tend to hold the interest of participants
    B. the format is often confusing for participants to follow
    C. it is perceived as being unfair
    D. it does not allow a participant to have an *off day*

36

7. When estimating the short-term recreational facility demand projections for a community, a manager should describe the agency's actions to be taken over the next _____ years.

   A. 1-2 B. 3-5 C. 5-10 D. 15

8. If the existence of an *attractive nuisance* can be proved, a park and recreation department can be found liable for an injury to a person who has illegally trespassed onto an unsupervised facility.
   Each of the following conditions is necessary in order to prove the existence of an *attractive nuisance* EXCEPT

   A. the trespasser is a child who is judged to be too young to know better
   B. the property is not completely enclosed by a fence at least 6 feet in height
   C. the agency or owner of the land upon which the child trespasses is aware that the area is attractive to children
   D. a dangerous condition exists on the property that is not a natural hazard

9. Within a working group, the degree to which a situation is favorable or unfavorable for the use of a task-oriented leadership style is MOST dependent on

   A. the quality of leader-member relationships
   B. task structure
   C. the size of the group
   D. the leader's position power

10. A park and recreation department leases a golf course to another agency. In terms of liability, the department is practicing risk

    A. avoidance   B. reduction
    C. transfer   D. retention

11. Cost accounting is useful to a park and recreation department in each of the following ways EXCEPT

    A. determining the proper balance between different phases of departmental operation
    B. evaluating individual personnel performance
    C. evaluating expenditures referenced to different elements of the community population
    D. determining the feasibility of constructing facilities with either the agency's own labor or on a contractual basis

12. The contract method of scheduling personnel in a park and recreation department is unrealistic when

    A. positions require specialization
    B. personnel qualifications and availability are consistent
    C. employees wish to select their own days and shifts
    D. the system requires the establishment of work schedules for a specific time span

13. In the personnel classification system traditionally used in public agencies such as park and recreation departments, supervisors are normally responsible for

    A. coordinating and directing the overall work of the department
    B. overseeing responsibilities within a geographical area or district of a community

C. planning, organizing, and directly supervising recreation programs in one or more facilities
D. recruiting, selecting, assigning, and supervising all department personnel

14. Which of the following steps in a municipal park planning procedure is generally performed FIRST?

    A. The preliminary design
    B. Inspection of the site with topographic map in hand
    C. The making of the investigative report
    D. Working drawings and specifications

15. When a manager or supervisor relies upon a(n) _____ style of leadership, the reaction of employees will most often be hostility and aggression within members of the group.

    A. laissez-faire   B. democratic
    C. authoritative   D. autocratic

16. Which of the following approaches to recreation program development is focused on the need to provide programs that are responsive to community pressures and influences?

    A. Traditional   B. Expressed desires
    C. Sociopolitical   D. Current practices

17. Risk retention is a valid policy for a park and recreation department under each of the following conditions EXCEPT when

    A. the maximum possible loss is so small that the agency can absorb it in the operating budget
    B. it is possible to transfer the risks to another
    C. the probability of a loss is so low that it can be ignored
    D. the cost to transfer the risk is so high that it would cost almost as much as the worst loss that could occur

18. Most public park and recreation department contracts with other organizations fall into several clearly defined categories. Which of the following is LEAST likely to be one of these?

    A. Direct programming and leadership of department services
    B. The purchase of equipment, materials, and supplies
    C. Planning, design, or construction of capital facilities
    D. Arrangements for concessions, franchises, or leases of special types of service or facilities

19. To make an agency's services more effective, supervision of staff should be thought of as a(n) _____ process.

    A. permissive   B. directing
    C. enabling   D. controlling

20. Which type of commercial leisure-service organizations account for the greatest dollar-volume of annual sales?

    A. Partnerships   B. Institutions
    C. Corporations   D. Sole proprietorships

21. In addition to public resistance to the implementation of a fee structure for certain services or facilities, a park and recreation department may encounter some administrative problems. Which of the following is NOT typically one of these problems?

    A. The fees may be illegal in some cases
    B. Difficulty in controlling access to services where fees are levied
    C. The exclusion of certain disadvantaged groups may present an unmanageable apparatus
    D. The cost of administering fees may be more than the revenues generated by it

21._____

22. When composing a grant proposal, which of the following pieces of information will probably be LEAST useful to the reader?

    A. Demonstration of critical need
    B. Capital facilities that can be used as collateral
    C. A precise statement of the budget
    D. Availability of matching funds

22._____

23. To be most effective in his or her leadership role, a manager in a park and recreation department should be each of the following EXCEPT

    A. optimistic   B. aggressive
    C. resilient   D. reactive

23._____

24. Recreation and park administrators should involve themselves as fully as possible in each construction project — according to each of the following guidelines EXCEPT

    A. become familiar with all background information related to the facility plan and be actively involved in all public hearings
    B. be present at the first design conference to make sure program needs are considered, and then obtaining a summary of each modification session
    C. insist that all construction details or standards be carried out exactly as specified
    D. visit the construction site regularly, once construction begins, either with staff members or with the architect

24._____

25. Volunteers at a park and recreation department are LEAST likely to assist in

    A. the budgeting process
    B. program delivery
    C. logistical services
    D. an administrative-advisory capacity

25._____

KEY (CORRECT ANSWERS)

1.	D	11.	C
2.	A	12.	A
3.	D	13.	B
4.	C	14.	C
5.	D	15.	D
6.	B	16.	C
7.	B	17.	B
8.	B	18.	A
9.	A	19.	C
10.	C	20.	C

21. C
22. B
23. D
24. B
25. A

EXAMINATION SECTION
TEST 1

DIRECTIONS: Each question or incomplete statement is followed by several suggested answers or completions. Select the one that BEST answers the question or completes the statement. *PRINT THE LETTER OF THE CORRECT ANSWER IN THE SPACE AT THE RIGHT.*

1. When conducting a needs assessment for the purpose of education planning, an agency's FIRST step is to identify or provide
    A. a profile of population characteristics
    B. barriers to participation
    C. existing resources
    D. profiles of competing resources

2. Research has demonstrated that of the following, the MOST effective medium for communicating with external publics is(are)
    A. video news releases
    B. television
    C. radio
    D. newspapers

3. Basic ideas behind the effort to influence the attitudes and behaviors of a constituency include each of the following EXCEPT the idea that
    A. words, rather than actions or events, are most likely to motivate
    B. demands for action are a usual response
    C. self-interest usually figures heavily into public involvement
    D. the reliability of change programs is difficult to assess

4. An agency representative is trying to craft a pithy message to constituents in order to encourage the use of agency program resources.
   Choosing an audience for such messages is easiest when the message
    A. is project- or behavior-based
    B. is combined with other messages
    C. is abstract
    D. has a broad appeal

5. Of the following factors, the MOST important to the success of an agency's external education or communication programs is the
    A. amount of resources used to implement them
    B. public's prior experiences with the agency
    C. real value of the program to the public
    D. commitment of the internal audience

6. A representative for a state agency is being interviewed by a reporter from a local news network. The representative is being asked to defend a program that is extremely unpopular in certain parts of the municipality.
   When a constituency is known to be opposed to a position, the MOST useful communication strategy is to present

A. only the arguments that are consistent with constituents' views
B. only the agency's side of the issue
C. both sides of the argument as clearly as possible
D. both sides of the argument, omitting key information about the opposing position

7. The MOST significant barriers to effective agency community relations include
   I. widespread distrust of communication strategies
   II. the media's "watchdog" stance
   III. public apathy
   IV. statutory opposition

   The CORRECT answer is:
   A. I only   B. I and II   C. II and III   D. III and IV

8. In conducting an education program, many agencies use workshops and seminars in a classroom setting.
   Advantages of classroom-style teaching over other means of educating the public include each of the following, EXCEPT
   A. enabling an instructor to verify learning through testing and interaction with the target audience
   B. enabling hands-on practice and other participatory learning techniques
   C. ability to reach an unlimited number of participants in a given length of time
   D. ability to convey the latest, most up-to-date information

9. The _____ model of community relations is characterized by an attempt to persuade the public to adopt the agency's point of view.
   A. two-way symmetric   B. two-way asymmetric
   C. public information   D. press agency/publicity

10. Important elements of an internal situation analysis include the
    I. list of agency opponents   II. communication audit
    III. updated organizational almanac   IV. stakeholder analysis

    The CORRECT answer is:
    A. I and II   B. I, II, and III   C. II and III   D. I, II, III and IV

11. Government agency information efforts typically involve each of the following objectives, EXCEPT to
    A. implement changes in the policies of government agencies to align with public opinion
    B. communicate the work of agencies
    C. explain agency techniques in a way that invites input from citizens
    D. provide citizen feedback to government administrators

12. Factors that are likely to influence the effectiveness of an educational campaign include the
    I. level of homogeneity among intended participants
    II. number and types of media used
    III. receptivity of the intended participants
    IV. level of specificity in the message or behavior to be taught

    The CORRECT answer is:
    A. I and II   B. I, II, and III   C. II and III   D. I, II, III, and IV

13. An agency representative is writing instructional objectives that will later help to measure the effectiveness of an educational program.
    Which of the following verbs, included in an objective, would be MOST helpful for the purpose of measuring effectiveness?
    A. Know   B. Identify   C. Learn   D. Comprehend

14. A state education agency wants to encourage participation in a program that has just received a boost through new federal legislation. The program is intended to include participants from a wide variety of socioeconomic and other demographic characteristics. The agency wants to launch a broad-based program that will inform virtually every interested party in the state about the program's new circumstances.
    In attempting to deliver this message to such a wide-ranging constituency, the agency's BEST practice would be to
    A. broadcast the same message through as many different media channels as possible
    B. focus on one discrete segment of the public at a time
    C. craft a message whose appeal is as broad as the public itself
    D. let the program's achievements speak for themselves and rely on word-of-mouth

15. Advantages associated with using the World Wide Web as an educational tool include
    I. an appeal to younger generations of the public
    II. visually-oriented, interactive learning
    III. learning that is not confined by space, time, or institutional association
    IV. a variety of methods for verifying use and learning

    The CORRECT answer is:
    A. I only   B. I and II   C. I, II, and III   D. I, II, II, and IV

16. In agencies involved in health care, community relations is a critical function because it
    A. serves as an intermediary between the agency and consumers
    B. generates a clear mission statement for agency goals and priorities
    C. ensures patient privacy while satisfying the media's right to information
    D. helps marketing professionals determine the wants and needs of agency constituents

17. After an extensive campaign to promote its newest program to constituents, an agency learns that most of the audience did not understand the intended message.
MOST likely, the agency has
   A. chosen words that were intended to inform, rather than persuade
   B. not accurately interpreted what the audience really needed to know
   C. overestimated the ability of the audience to receive and process the message
   D. compensated for noise that may have interrupted the message

18. The necessary elements that lead to conviction and motivation in the minds of participants in an educational or information program include each of the following, EXCEPT the _____ of the message.
   A. acceptability   B. intensity
   C. single-channel appeal   D. pervasiveness

19. Printed materials are often at the core of educational programs provided by public agencies.
The PRIMARY disadvantage associated with print is that it
   A. does not enable comprehensive treatment of a topic
   B. is generally unreliable in term of assessing results
   C. is often the most expensive medium available
   D. is constrained by time

20. Traditional thinking on public opinion holds that there is about _____ percent of the public who are pivotal to shifting the balance and momentum of opinion—they are concerned about an issue, but not fanatical, and interested enough to pay attention to a reasoned discussion.
   A. 2   B. 10   C. 33   D. 51

21. One of the most useful guidelines for influencing attitude change among people is to
   A. invite the target audience to come to you, rather than approaching them
   B. use moral appeals as the primary approach
   C. use concrete images to enable people to see the results of behaviors or indifference
   D. offer tangible rewards to people for changes in behavior

22. An agency is attempting to evaluate the effectiveness of its educational program. For this purpose, it wants to observe several focus groups discussing the same program.
Which of the following would NOT be a guideline for the use of focus groups?
   A. Focus groups should only include those who have participated in the program.
   B. Be sure to accurately record the discussion.
   C. The same questions should be asked at each focus group meeting.
   D. It is often helpful to have a neutral, non-agency employee facilitate discussions.

23. Research consistently shows that _____ is the determinant most likely to make a newspaper editor run a news release.
    A. novelty B. prominence C. proximity D. conflict

24. Which of the following is NOT one of the major variables to take into account when considering a population-needs assessment?
    A. State of program development B. Resources available
    C. Demographics D. Community attitudes

25. The FIRST step in any communications audit is to
    A. develop a research instrument
    B. determine how the organization currently communicates
    C. hire a contractor
    D. determine which audience to assess

KEY (CORRECT ANSWERS)

1.	A	11.	A
2.	D	12.	D
3.	A	13.	B
4.	A	14.	B
5.	D	15.	C
6.	C	16.	A
7.	D	17.	B
8.	C	18.	C
9.	B	19.	B
10.	C	20.	B

21. C
22. A
23. C
24. C
25. D

TEST 2

DIRECTIONS: Each question or incomplete statement is followed by several suggested answers or completions. Select the one that BEST answers the question or completes the statement. *PRINT THE LETTER OF THE CORRECT ANSWER IN THE SPACE AT THE RIGHT.*

1. A public relations practitioner at an agency has just composed a press release highlighting a program's recent accomplishments and success stories. In pitching such releases to print outlets, the practitioner should
   I. e-mail, mail, or send them by messenger
   II. address them to "editor" or "news director"
   III. have an assistant call all media contacts by telephone
   IV. ask reporters or editors how they prefer to receive them

   The CORRECT answer is:
   A. I and II   B. I and IV   C. II, III, and IV   D. III only

   1._____

2. The "output goals" of an educational program are MOST likely to include
   A. specified ratings of services by participants on a standardized scale
   B. observable effects on a given community or clientele
   C. the number of instructional hours provided
   D. the number of participants served

   2._____

3. An agency wants to evaluate satisfaction levels among program participants, and mails out questionnaires to everyone who has been enrolled in the last year.
   The PRIMARY problem associated with this method of evaluative research is that it
   A. poses a significant inconvenience for respondents
   B. is inordinately expensive
   C. does not allow for follow-up or clarification questions
   D. usually involves a low response rate

   3._____

4. A communications audit is an important tool for measuring
   A. the depth of penetration of a particular message or program
   B. the cost of the organization's information campaigns
   C. how key audiences perceive an organization
   D. the commitment of internal stakeholders

   4._____

5. The "ABCs" of written learning objectives include each of the following, EXCEPT
   A. Audience   B. Behavior   C. Conditions   D. Delineation

   5._____

6. When attempting to change the behaviors of constituents, it is important to keep in mind that
   I. most people are skeptical of communications that try to get them to change their behaviors
   II. in most cases, a person selects the media to which he exposes himself
   III. people tend to react defensively to messages or programs that rely on fear as a motivating factor
   IV. programs should aim for the broadest appeal possible in order to include as many participants as possible

   The CORRECT answer is:
   A. I and II   B. I, II and III   C. II and III   D. I, II, III, and IV

7. The "laws" of public opinion include the idea that it is
   A. useful for anticipating emergencies
   B. not sensitive to important events
   C. basically determined by self-interest
   D. sustainable through persistent appeals

8. Which of the following types of evaluations is used to measure public attitudes before and after an information/educational program?
   A. Retrieval study
   B. Copy test
   C. Quota sampling
   D. Benchmark study

9. The PRIMARY source for internal communications is(are) usually
   A. flow charts
   B. meetings
   C. voice mail
   D. printed publications

10. An agency representative is putting together informational materials—brochures and a newsletter—outlining changes in one of the state's biggest benefits programs.
    In assembling print materials as a medium for delivering information to the public, the representative should keep in mind each of the following trends:
    I. For various reasons, the reading capabilities of the public are in general decline
    II. Without tables and graphs to help illustrate the changes, it is unlikely that the message will be delivered effectively
    III. Professionals and career-oriented people are highly receptive to information written in the form of a journal article or empirical study
    IV. People tend to be put off by print materials that use itemized and bulleted (●) lists

    The CORRECT answer is:
    A. I and II   B. I, II and III   C. II and III   D. I, II, III, and IV

11. Which of the following steps in a problem-oriented information campaign would typically be implemented FIRST?
    A. Deciding on tactics
    B. Determining a communications strategy
    C. Evaluating the problem's impact
    D. Developing an organizational strategy

11.____

12. A common pitfall in conducting an educational program is to
    A. aim it at the wrong target audience
    B. overfund it
    C. leave it in the hands of people who are in the business of education, rather than those with expertise in the business of the organization
    D. ignore the possibility that some other organization is meeting the same educational need for the target audience

12.____

13. The key factors that affect the credibility of an agency's educational program include
    A. organization   B. scope
    C. sophistication   D. penetration

13.____

14. Research on public opinion consistently demonstrates that it is
    A. easy to move people toward a strong opinion on anything, as long as they are approached directly through their emotions
    B. easier to move people away from an opinion they currently hold than to have them form an opinion about something they have not previously cared about
    C. easy to move people toward a strong opinion on anything, as long as the message appeals to their reason and intellect
    D. difficult to move people toward a strong opinion on anything, no matter what the approach

14.____

15. In conducting an education program, many agencies use meetings and conferences to educate an audience about the organization and its programs. Advantages associated with this approach include
    I. a captive audience that is known to be interested in the topic
    II. ample opportunities for verifying learning
    III. cost-efficient meeting space
    IV. the ability to provide information on a wider variety of subjects

    The CORRECT answer is:
    A. I and II   B. I, III and IV   C. II and III   D. I, II, III and IV

15.____

16. An agency is attempting to evaluate the effectiveness of its educational programs. For this purpose, it wants to observe several focus groups discussing particular programs.
    For this purpose, a focus group should never number more than _____ participants.
    A. 5   B. 10   C. 15   D. 20

16.____

17. A _____ speech is written so that several agency members can deliver it to different audiences with only minor variations.
    A. basic   B. printed   C. quota   D. pattern

18. Which of the following statements about public opinion is generally considered to be FALSE?
    A. Opinion is primarily reactive rather than proactive.
    B. People have more opinions about goals than about the means by which to achieve them.
    C. Facts tend to shift opinion in the accepted direction when opinion is not solidly structured.
    D. Public opinion is based more on information than desire.

19. An agency is trying to promote its educational program.
    As a general rule, the agency should NOT assume that
    A. people will only participate if they perceive an individual benefit
    B. promotions need to be aimed at small, discrete groups
    C. if the program is good, the audience will find out about it
    D. a variety of methods, including advertising, special events, and direct mail, should be considered

20. In planning a successful educational program, probably the first and most important question for an agency to ask is:
    A. What will be the content of the program?
    B. Who will be served by the program?
    C. When is the best time to schedule the program?
    D. Why is the program necessary?

21. Media kits are LEAST likely to contain
    A. fact sheets   B. memoranda
    C. photographs with captions   D. news releases

22. The use of pamphlets and booklets as media for communication with the public often involves the disadvantage that
    A. the messages contained within them are frequently nonspecific
    B. it is difficult to measure their effectiveness in delivering the message
    C. there are few opportunities for people to refer to them
    D. color reproduction is poor

23. The MOST important prerequisite of a good educational program is an
    A. abundance of resources to implement it
    B. individual staff unit formed for the purpose of program delivery
    C. accurate needs assessment
    D. uneducated constituency

24. After an education program has been delivered, an agency conducts a program evaluation to determine whether its objectives have been met.
General rules about how to conduct such an education program valuation include each of the following, EXCEPT that it
    A. must be done immediately after the program has been implemented
    B. should be simple and easy to use
    C. should be designed so that tabulation of responses can take place quickly and inexpensively
    D. should solicit mostly subjective, open-ended responses if the audience was large

25. Using electronic media such as television as means of educating the public is typically recommended ONLY for agencies that
    I. have a fairly simple message to begin with
    II. want to reach the masses, rather than a targeted audience
    III. have substantial financial resources
    IV. accept that they will not be able to measure the results of the campaign with much precision

    The CORRECT answer is:
    A. I and II   B. I, II and III   C. II and IV   D. I, II, III and IV

KEY (CORRECT ANSWERS)

1. B
2. C
3. D
4. C
5. D

6. B
7. C
8. D
9. D
10. A

11. C
12. D
13. A
14. D
15. B

16. B
17. D
18. D
19. C
20. D

21. B
22. B
23. C
24. D
25. D

EXAMINATION SECTION
TEST 1

DIRECTIONS: Each question or incomplete statement is followed by several suggested answers or completions. Select the one that BEST answers the question or completes the statement. *PRINT THE LETTER OF THE CORRECT ANSWER IN THE SPACE AT THE RIGHT.*

1. The budget which shows the money to be spent to build and equip a new hospital is known as the _____ budget.

    A. capital   B. expense   C. planned   D. program

2. A significant characteristic of the program budget is that it lends itself to review and analysis.
   Why?

    A. The budget has a built-in accounting system that makes close control possible.
    B. The budget includes measurable objectives.
    C. It is possible to review performance based on units of service.
    D. All of the above

3. The advantages of program budgeting over line item and performance budgeting is:
     I. Tight, administrative control
     II. Forces the administrator to think through his total operation
     III. Measurable objectives
     IV. Simplicity of development
     V. Closer estimates of future costs
   The CORRECT answer is:

    A. I, II
    B. II, III, IV
    C. II, III, V
    D. III, IV, V

4. Of the following considerations, the one which is LEAST important in preparing a department budget request is the

    A. amounts in previous budget requests
    B. cost of material
    C. cost of personnel
    D. goals of the agency

5. The type of budget which provides the MOST flexibility in the use of appropriate funds is the _____ budget.

    A. accrual   B. item   C. line   D. program

6. A WEAKNESS of many budgetary systems today is that they

    A. are subjectively determined by those most directly involved
    B. focus on management weakness rather than management strength
    C. only show variable costs
    D. show in detail why losses are occurring

7. Standards on which budgets are developed should be based PRIMARILY on

   A. a general consensus
   B. agency wishes
   C. analytical studies
   D. historical performance

8. The income, cost, and expense goals making up a budget are aimed at achieving a predetermined objective but do not necessarily measure the lowest possible costs.
   This is PRIMARILY so because

   A. budget committees are accounting-oriented and are not sympathetic with the supervisor's personnel problems
   B. budget committees fail to recognize the difference between direct and indirect costs
   C. the level of expenditures provided for in a budget by budget committees is frequently an arbitrary rather than a scientifically determined amount
   D. budget committees spend considerable time evaluating data to the point that the material gathered is not representative or current

9. You, as a unit head, have been asked to submit budget estimates of staff, equipment, and supplies in terms of programs for your unit for the coming fiscal year.
   In addition to their use in planning, such unit budget estimates can be BEST used to

   A. reveal excessive costs in operations
   B. justify increases in the debt limit
   C. analyze employee salary adjustments
   D. predict the success of future programs

10. Which of the following is the BEST reason for budgeting a new calculating machine for an office?

    A. The clerks in the office often make mistakes in adding.
    B. The machine would save time and money.
    C. It was budgeted last year but never received.
    D. All the other offices have calculating machines.

11. As an aspect of the managerial function, a budget is described BEST as a

    A. set of qualitative management controls over productivity
    B. tool based on historical accounting reports
    C. type of management plan expressed in quantitative terms
    D. precise estimate of future quantitative and qualitative contingencies

12. Which one of the following is *generally* accepted as the MAJOR immediate advantage of installing a system of program budgeting? It

    A. encourages managers to relate their decisions to the agency's long-range goals
    B. is a replacement for the financial or fiscal budget
    C. decreases the need for managers to make trade-offs in the decision-making process
    D. helps to adjust budget figures to provide for unexpected developments

13. Of the following, the BEST means for assuring necessary responsiveness of a budgetary program to changing conditions is by

    A. overestimating budgetary expenditures by 15% and assigning the excess to unforeseen problem areas
    B. underestimating budgetary expenditures by at least 20% and setting aside a reserve account in the same amount
    C. reviewing and revising the budget at regular intervals so that it retains its character as a current document
    D. establishing *budget by exception* policies for each division in the agency

14. According to expert thought in the area of budgeting, participation in the preparation of a government agency's budget should GENERALLY involve

    A. only top management
    B. only lower levels of management
    C. all levels of the organization
    D. only a central budget office or bureau

15. Of the following, the MOST useful guide to analysis of budget estimates for the coming fiscal year is a comparison with

    A. appropriations as amended for the current fiscal year
    B. manpower requirements for the previous two years
    C. initial appropriations for the current fiscal year
    D. budget estimates for the preceding five years,

16. Line managers often request more funds for their units than are actually required to attain their current objectives.
    Which one of the following is the MOST important reason for such inflated budget requests? The

    A. expectation that budget examiners will exercise their prerogative of budget cutting
    B. line manager's interest in improving the performance of his unit is thereby indicated to top management
    C. expectation that such requests will make it easier to obtain additional funds in future years
    D. opinion that it makes sense to obtain additional funds and decide later how to use them

17. Integrating budgeting with program planning and evaluation in a city agency is GENERALLY considered to be

    A. *undesirable*; budgeting must focus on the fiscal year at hand, whereas planning must concern itself with developments over a period of years
    B. *desirable*; budgeting facilitates the choice-making process by evaluating the financial implications of agency programs and forcing cost comparisons among them
    C. *undesirable*; accountants and statisticians with the required budgetary skills have little familiarity with the substantive programs that the agency is conducting
    D. *desirable*; such a partnership increases the budgetary skills of planners, thus promoting more effective use of public resources

18. In government budgeting, the problem of relating financial transactions to the fiscal year in which they are budgeted is BEST met by

    A. determining the cash balance by comparing how much money has been received and how much has been paid out
    B. applying net revenue to the fiscal year in which they are collected as offset by relevant expenses
    C. adopting a system whereby appropriations are entered when they are received and expenditures are entered when they are paid out
    D. entering expenditures on the books when the obligation to make the expenditure is made

19. If the agency's bookkeeping system records income when it is received and expenditures when the money is paid out, this system is USUALLY known as a _____ system.

    A. cash
    B. flow-payment
    C. deferred
    D. fiscal year income

20. An audit, as the term applies to budget execution, is MOST NEARLY a

    A. procedure based on the budget estimates
    B. control exercised by the executive on the legislature in the establishment of program priorities
    C. check on the legality of expenditures and is based on the appropriations act
    D. requirement which must be met before funds can be spent

21. In government budgeting, there is a procedure known as *allotment.*
    Of the following statements which relate to allotment, select the one that is MOST generally considered to be correct. Allotment

    A. increases the practice of budget units coming back to the legislative branch for supplemental appropriations
    B. is simply an example of red tape
    C. eliminates the requirement of timing of expenditures
    D. is designed to prevent waste

22. In government budgeting, the establishment of the schedules of allotments is MOST generally the responsibility of the

    A. budget unit and the legislature
    B. budget unit and the executive
    C. budget unit only
    D. executive and the legislature

23. Of the following statements relating to preparation of an organization's budget request, which is the MOST generally valid precaution?

    A. Give specific instructions on the format of budget requests and required supporting data.
    B. Because of the complexity of preparing a budget request, avoid argumentation to support the requests.
    C. Put requests in whatever format is desirable.
    D. Consider that final approval will be given to initial estimates.

Question 24.

DIRECTIONS: Answer Question 24 on the basis of the following information.

<u>Sample Budget</u>

Environmental Safety
   Air Pollution Protection
      Personal Services $20,000,000
      Contractual Services   4,000,000
      Supplies and Materials   4,000,000
      Capital Outlay   2,000,000
        Total Air Pollution Protection $30,000,000

   Water Pollution Protection
      Personal Services $23,000,000
      Supplies and Materials   4,500,000
      Capital Outlay   20,500,000
        Total Water Pollution Protection $48,000,000
Total Environmental Safety $78,000,000

24. Based on the above budget, which is the MOST valid statement?

   A. Environmental Safety, Air Pollution Protection, and Water Pollution Protection could all be considered program elements.
   B. The object listings included water pollution protection and capital outlay.
   C. Examples of the program element listings in the above are personal services and supplies and materials.
   D. Contractual Services and Environmental Safety were the program element listings.

25. Which of the following is NOT an advantage of a program budget over a line-item budget?
A program budget

   A. allows us to set up priority lists in deciding what activities we will spend our money on
   B. gives us more control over expenditures than a line-item budget
   C. is more informative in that we know the broad purposes of spending money
   D. enables us to see if one program is getting much less money than the others

26. Of the following statements which relate to the budget process in a well-organized government, select the one that is MOST NEARLY correct.

   A. The budget cycle is the step-by-step process which is repeated each and every fiscal year.
   B. Securing approval of the budget does not take place within the budget cycle.
   C. The development of a new budget and putting it into effect is a two-step process known as the budget cycle.
   D. The fiscal period, usually a fiscal year, has no relation to the budget cycle.

27. If a manager were asked what PPBS stands for, he would be right if he said

   A. public planning budgeting system
   B. planning programming budgeting system
   C. planning projections budgeting system
   D. programming procedures budgeting system

Questions 28-29

DIRECTIONS: Answer Questions 28 and 29 on the basis of the following information.

Sample Budget

	Amount
Refuse Collection	
Personal Services	$ 30,000
Contractual Services	5,000
Supplies and Materials	5,000
Capital Outlay	10,000
	$ 50,000
Residential Collections	
Dwellings—1 pickup per week	1,000
Tons of refuse collected per year	375
Cost of collections per ton	$ 8
Cost per dwelling pickup per year	$ 3
Total annual cost	$ 3,000

28. The sample budget shown is a simplified example of a _____ budget.

   A. factorial   B. performance
   C. qualitative   D. rational

29. The budget shown in the sample differs CHIEFLY from line-item and program budgets in that it includes

   A. objects of expenditure but not activities or functions
   B. only activities, functions, and controls
   C. activities and functions, but not objects of expenditure
   D. levels of service

30. Performance budgeting focuses PRIMARY attention upon which one of the following? The

   A. things to be acquired, such as supplies and equipment
   B. general character and relative importance of the work to be done or the service to be rendered
   C. list of personnel to be employed, by specific title
   D. separation of employee performance evaluations from employee compensation

KEY (CORRECT ANSWERS)

1.	A	16.	A
2.	B	17.	B
3.	C	18.	D
4.	A	19.	A
5.	D	20.	C
6.	A	21.	D
7.	C	22.	C
8.	C	23.	A
9.	A	24.	A
10.	B	25.	B
11.	C	26.	A
12.	A	27.	B
13.	C	28.	B
14.	C	29.	D
15.	A	30.	B

TEST 2

DIRECTIONS: Each question or incomplete statement is followed by several suggested answers or completions. Select the one that BEST answers the question or completes the statement. *PRINT THE LETTER OF THE CORRECT ANSWER IN THE SPACE AT THE RIGHT.*

1. Of the following, the FIRST step in the installation and operation of a performance budgeting system generally should be the

    A. identification of program costs in relationship to the accounting system and operating structure
    B. identification of the specific end results of past programs in other jurisdictions
    C. identification of work programs that are meaningful for management purposes
    D. establishment of organizational structures each containing only one work program

   1.____

2. Of the following, the MOST important purpose of a system of quarterly allotments of appropriated funds generally is to enable the

    A. head of the judicial branch to determine the legality of agency requests for budget increases
    B. operating agencies of government to upgrade the quality of their services without increasing costs
    C. head of the executive branch to control the rate at which the operating agencies obligate and expend funds
    D. operating agencies of government to avoid payment for services which have not been properly rendered by employees

   2.____

3. In the preparation of the agency's budget, the agency's central budget office has two responsibilities: program review and management improvement.
   Which one of the following questions concerning an operating agency's program is MOST closely related to the agency budget officer's program review responsibility?

    A. Can expenditures for supplies, materials, or equipment be reduced?
    B. Will improved work methods contribute to a more effective program?
    C. What is the relative importance of this program as compared with other programs?
    D. Will a realignment of responsibilities contribute to a higher level of program performance?

   3.____

Questions 4-9.

DIRECTIONS: Questions 4 through 9 are to be answered only on the basis of the information contained in the charts below which relate to the budget allocations of City X, a small suburban community. The charts depict the annual budget allocations by Department and by Expenditures over a five-year period.

CITY X BUDGET IN MILLIONS OF DOLLARS

TABLE I.   Budget Allocations by Department

Department	2017	2018	2019	2020	2021
Public Safety	30	45	50	40	50
Health and Welfare	50	75	90	60	70
Engineering	5	8	10	5	8
Human Resources	10	12	20	10	22
Conservation and Environment	10	15	20	20	15
Education and Development	15	25	35	15	15
TOTAL BUDGET	120	180	225	150	180

TABLE II.   Budget Allocations by Expenditures

Category	2017	2018	2019	2020	2021
Raw Materials and Machinery	36	63	68	30	98
Capital Outlay	12	27	56	15	18
Personal Services	72	90	101	105	64
TOTAL BUDGET	120	180	225	150	160

4. The year in which the SMALLEST percentage of the total annual budget was allocated to the Department of Education and Development is

   A. 2017   B. 2018   C. 2020   D. 2021

5. Assume that in 2020 the Department of Conservation and Environment divided its annual budget into the three categories of expenditures and in exactly the same proportion as the budget shown in Table II for the year 2020. The amount allocated for capital outlay in the Department of Conservation and Environment's 2020 budget was MOST NEARLY _____ million.

   A. $2   B. $4   C. $6   D. $10

6. From the year 2018 to the year 2020, the sum of the annual budgets for the Departments of Public Safety and Engineering showed an overall _____ million.

   A. decline of $8
   B. increase of $7
   C. decline of $15
   D. increase of $22

7. The LARGEST dollar increase in departmental budget allocations from one year to the next was in

   A. Public Safety from 2017 to 2018
   B. Health and Welfare from 2017 to 2018
   C. Education and Development from 2019 to 2020
   D. Human Resources from 2019 to 2020

8. During the five-year period, the annual budget of the Department of Human Resources was greater than the annual budget for the Department of Conservation and Environment in _____ of the years.

   A. none   B. one   C. two   D. three

9. If the total City X budget increases at the same rate from 2021 to 2022 as it did from 2020 to 2021, the total City X budget for 2022 will be MOST NEARLY _____ million.

   A. $180 B. $200 C. $210 D. $215

10. The one of the following which is LEAST important in developing a budget for the next fiscal year for project maintenance is the

    A. adequacy of the current year's budget
    B. changes in workload that can be anticipated
    C. budget restrictions indicated in a memorandum covering budget preparations
    D. staff reassignments which are expected during the next fiscal year

11. The performance budget used by the department places MOST emphasis on

    A. building facilities
    B. equipment costs
    C. personnel costs
    D. services rendered

12. The LARGEST part of the expenditures of the department is for

    A. equipment
    B. maintenance
    C. operating materials
    D. personnel services

13. The department function which requires the GREATEST expenditure of funds is

    A. refuse collection
    B. refuse disposal
    C. snow removal
    D. street cleaning

14. A FIRST step in budget preparation is *usually*

    A. a realistic attempt to satisfy all unit requests
    B. forecasting the amount of various kinds of work to be done during the coming budget year
    C. an effort to increase work output
    D. appraising the quality of work done in the previous year

15. There are various types of budgets which are used to measure different government activities.
    The type of budget which *particularly* measures input of resource as compared with output of service is the _____ budget.

    A. capital B. traditional C. performance D. program

16. The budget for a given cost during a given period was $100,000. The actual cost for the period was $90,000. Based upon these facts, one should say that the responsible manager has done a better than expected job in controlling the cost if the cost is

    A. variable and actual production equaled budgeted production
    B. a discretionary fixed cost and actual production equaled budgeted production
    C. variable and actual production was 90% of budgeted production
    D. variable and actual production was 80% of budgeted production

17. In most municipal budgeting systems involving capital and operating budgets, the leasing or renting of facilities is usually shown in

    A. the operating budget
    B. the capital budget
    C. a separate schedule
    D. either budget

18. New York City's budgeting procedure is unusual in that budget appropriations are considered in two parts, as follows: _____ budget and _____ budget.

    A. capital; income
    B. expense; income
    C. revenue; expense
    D. expense; capital

19. Budget planning is MOST useful when it achieves

    A. cost control
    B. forecast of receipts
    C. performance review
    D. personnel reduction

20. After a budget has been developed, it serves to

    A. assist the accounting department in posting expenditures
    B. measure the effectiveness of department managers
    C. provide a yardstick against which actual costs are measured
    D. provide the operating department with total expenditures to date

21. A budget is a plan whereby a goal is set for future operations. It affords a medium for comparing actual expenditures with planned expenditures.
    The one of the following which is the MOST accurate statement on the basis of this statement is that

    A. the budget serves as an accurate measure of past as well as future expenditures
    B. the budget presents an estimate of expenditures to be made in the future
    C. budget estimates should be based upon past budget requirements
    D. planned expenditures usually fall short of actual expenditures

22. If one attempts to list the advantages of the management-by-exception principle as it is used in connection with the budgeting process, several distinct advantages could be cited.
    Which of the following is NOT an advantage of this principle as it applies to the budgeting process? Management-by-exception

    A. saves time
    B. identifies critical problem areas
    C. focuses attention and concentrates effort
    D. escalates the frequency and importance of budget-related decisions

23. Of the following statements that relate to a budget, select the one that is MOST accurate.

    A. A budget is made up by an organization to plan its future activities.
    B. A budget specifies how much the organization to which it relates estimates it will spend over a certain period of time.
    C. A budget specifies in dollars and cents how much is spent in a particular time period.
    D. All plans dealing with money are budgets.

24. Of the following, the one which is NOT a contribution that a budget makes to organizational programming is that a budget

    A. enables a comparison of what actually happened with what was expected
    B. stresses the need to forecast specific goals and eliminates the need to focus on tasks needed to accomplish goals
    C. may illustrate duplication of effort between interdependent activities
    D. shows the relationship between various organizational segments

25. A line-item budget is a GOOD control budget because

    A. it clearly specifies how the items being purchased will be used
    B. expenditures can be shown primarily for contractual services
    C. it clearly specifies what the money is buying
    D. it clearly specifies the services to be provide

KEY (CORRECT ANSWERS)

1. C	11. D
2. C	12. D
3. C	13. A
4. D	14. B
5. A	15. C
6. A	16. A
7. B	17. A
8. B	18. D
9. D	19. A
10. D	20. C

21. B
22. D
23. B
24. B
25. C

EXAMINATION SECTION
TEST 1

DIRECTIONS: Each question or incomplete statement is followed by several suggested answers or completions. Select the one that BEST answers the question or completes the statement. *PRINT THE LETTER OF THE CORRECT ANSWER IN THE SPACE AT THE RIGHT.*

1. Assume that a manager is preparing a list of reasons to justify making a major change in methods and procedures in his agency.
    Which of the following reasons would be LEAST appropriate on such a list?
    A. Improve the means for satisfying needs and wants of agency personnel
    B. Increase efficiency
    C. Intensify competition and stimulate loyalty to separate work groups
    D. Contribute to the individual and group satisfaction of agency personnel

2. Many managers recognize the benefits of decentralization but are concerned about the danger of over-relaxation of control as a result of increased delegation.
    Of the following, the MOST appropriate means of establishing proper control under decentralization is for the manager to
    A. establish detailed standards for all phases of operation
    B. shift his attention from operating details to appraisal of results
    C. keep himself informed by decreasing the time span covered by reports
    D. make unilateral decisions on difficult situations that arise in decentralized locations

3. In some agencies, the counsel to the agency head is given the right to bypass the chain of command and issue orders directly to the staff concerning matters that involve certain specific processes and practices.
    This situation MOST NEARLY illustrates the principle of _____ authority.
    A. the acceptance theory of   B. multiple-linear
    C. splintered   D. functional

4. Assume that a manager is writing a brief report to his superior outlining the advantages of matrix organization.
    Of the following, it would be INCORRECT to state that
    A. in matrix organization, a project is emphasized by designating one individual as the focal point for all matters pertaining to it
    B. utilization of manpower can be flexible in matrix organization because a reservoir of specialists is maintained in the line operations
    C. the usual line staff arrangement is generally reversed in matrix organization
    D. in matrix organization, responsiveness to project needs is generally faster due to establishing needed communication lines and decision points

5. It is commonly understood that communication is an important part of the administrative process.
   Which of the following is NOT a valid principle of the communication process in administration?
   A. The channels of communication should be spontaneous.
   B. The lines of communication should be as direct and as short as possible.
   C. Communications should be authenticated.
   D. The persons serving in communications centers should be competent.

6. The PRIMARY purpose of the quantitative approach in management is to
   A. identify better alternatives for management decision-making
   B. substitute data for judgment
   C. match opinions to data
   D. match data to opinions

7. If an executive wants to make a strong case for running his agency as a flat type of structure, he should point out that the PRIMARY advantage of doing so is to
   A. provide less experience in decision-making for agency personnel
   B. facilitate frequent contact between each superior and his immediate subordinates
   C. improve communication and unify attitudes
   D. improve communication and diversify attitudes

8. In deciding how detailed his delegation of authority to a subordinate should be, a manager should follow the general principle that
   A. delegation of authority is more detailed at the top of the organizational structure
   B. detailed delegation of authority is associated with detailed work assignments
   C. delegation of authority should be in sufficient detail to prevent overlapping assignments
   D. detailed delegation of authority is associated with broad work assignments

9. In recent years, newer and more fluid types of organizational forms have been developed. One of these is a type of free-form organization.
   Another name for this type of organization is the
   A. project organization   B. semimix organization
   C. naturalistic structure   D. semipermanent structure

10. Which of the following is the MAJOR objective of operational or management systems audits?
    A. Determining the number of personnel needed
    B. Recommending opportunities for improving operating and management practices
    C. Detecting fraud
    D. Determining organization problems

11. Assume that a manager observes that conflict exists between his agency and another operating agency of government.
    Which of the following statements is the LEAST probable cause of this conflict?
    A. Incompatibility between the agencies' goals but similarity in their resource allocations
    B. Compatibility between agencies' goals and resources
    C. Status differences between agency personnel
    D. Differences in perceptions of each other's policies

12. Of the following, a MAJOR purpose of brainstorming as a problem-solving technique is to
    A. develop the ability to concentrate
    B. encourage creative thinking
    C. evaluate employees' ideas
    D. develop critical ability

13. The one of the following requirements which is LEAST likely to accompany regular delegation of work from a manager to a subordinate is a(n)
    A. need to review the organization's workload
    B. indication of what work the subordinate is to do
    C. need to grant authority to the subordinate
    D. obligation for the subordinate who accepts the work to try to complete it

14. Of the following, the one factor which is generally considered LEAST essential to successful committee operation is
    A. stating a clear definition of the authority and scope of the committee
    B. selecting the committee chairman carefully
    C. limiting the size of the committee to four persons
    D. limiting the subject matter to that which can be handled in group discussion

15. In using the program evaluation and review technique, the *critical path* is the path that
    A. requires the shortest time
    B. requires the longest time
    C. focuses most attention on social constraints
    D. focuses most attention to repetitious jobs

16. Which one of the following is LEAST characteristic of the management-by-objectives approach?
    A. The scope within which the employee may exercise decision-making is broadened.
    B. The employee starts with a self-appraisal of his performances, abilities, and potential.
    C. Emphasis is placed on activities performed; activities orientation is maximized.
    D. Each employee participates in determining his own objectives.

17. The function of management which puts into effect the decisions, plans, and programs that have previously been worked out for achieving the goals of the group is MOST appropriately called
    A. scheduling   B. classifying   C. budgeting   D. directing

18. In the establishment of a plan to improve office productive efficiency, which of the following guidelines is LEAST helpful in setting sound work standards?
    A. Employees must accept the plan's objectives.
    B. Current production averages must be promulgated as work standards for a group.
    C. The work flow must generally be fairly constant.
    D. The operation of the plan must be expressed in terms understandable to the worker.

19. The one of the following activities which, generally speaking, is of *relatively* MAJOR importance at the lower-management level and of *somewhat* LESSER importance at higher-management levels is
    A. actuating   B. forecasting   C. organizing   D. planning

20. Three styles of leadership exist: democratic, authoritarian, and laissez-faire. Of the following work situations, the one in which a democratic approach would normally be the MOST effective is when the work is
    A. routine and moderately complex   B. repetitious and simple
    C. complex and not routine   D. simple and not routine

21. Governmental and business organizations *generally* encounter the GREATEST difficulties in developing tangible measures of which one of the following?
    A. The level of expenditures   B. Contributions to social welfare
    C. Retention rates   D. Causes of labor unrest

22. Of the following, a *management-by-objectives* program is BEST described as
    A. a new comprehensive plan of organization
    B. introduction of budgets and financial controls
    C. introduction of long-range planning
    D. development of future goals with supporting and related progress reviews

23. Research and analysis is probably the most widely used technique for selecting alternatives when major planning decisions are involved.
    Of the following, a VALUABLE characteristic of research and analysis is that this technique
    A. places the problem in a meaningful conceptual framework
    B. involves practical application of the various alternatives
    C. accurately analyzes all important tangibles
    D. is much less expensive than other problem-solving methods

24. If a manager were assigned the task of using a systems approach to designing a new work unit, which of the following should he consider FIRST in carrying out his design?
    A. Networks
    B. Work flows and information processes
    C. Linkages and relationships
    D. Decision points and control loops

24.____

25. The MAIN distinction between Theory X and Theory Y approaches to organization, in accordance with Douglas McGregor's view, is that Theory Y
    A. considers that work is natural to people; Theory X assumes that people are lazy and avoid work
    B. leads to a tall, narrow organization structure, while Theory X leads to one that is flat
    C. organizations motivate people with money; Theory X organizations motivate people with good working conditions
    D. represents authoritarian management, while Theory X management is participative

25.____

KEY (CORRECT ANSWERS)

1.	C		11.	B
2.	B		12.	B
3.	D		13.	A
4.	C		14.	C
5.	A		15.	B
6.	A		16.	C
7.	C		17.	D
8.	B		18.	B
9.	A		19.	A
10.	B		20.	C

21.	B
22.	D
23.	A
24.	B
25.	A

TEST 2

DIRECTIONS: Each question or incomplete statement is followed by several suggested answers or completions. Select the one that BEST answers the question or completes the statement. *PRINT THE LETTER OF THE CORRECT ANSWER IN THE SPACE AT THE RIGHT.*

1. Of the following, the stage in decision-making which is usually MOST difficult is
   A. stating the alternatives
   B. predicting the possible outcome of each alternative
   C. evaluating the relative merits of each alternative
   D. minimizing the undesirable aspects of the alternative selected

   1.____

2. In a department where a clerk is reporting both to a senior clerk in charge of the mail room and also to a supervising clerk in charge of the duplicating section, there may be a breakdown of the management principle called
   A. horizontal specialization   B. job enrichment
   C. unity of command   D. Graicunas' Law

   2.____

3. Of the following, the failure by line managers to accept and appreciate the benefits and limitations of a new program or system VERY frequently can be traced to the
   A. budgetary problems involved
   B. resultant need to reduce staff
   C. lack of controls it engenders
   D. failure of top management to support its implementation

   3.____

4. Although there is general agreement that *management-by-objectives* has made a major contribution to modern management of large organizations, criticisms of the system during the past few years have resulted in
   A. mounting pressure for relaxation of management goals
   B. renewed concern with human values and the manager's personal needs
   C. over-mechanistic application of the perceptions of the behavioral scientists
   D. disillusionment with *management-by-objectives* on the part of a majority of managers

   4.____

5. Of the following, which is usually considered to be a MAJOR obstacle to the systematic analysis of potential problems by managers?
   A. Managers have a tendency to think that all the implications of some proposed step cannot be fully understood.
   B. Rewards rarely go to those managers who are most successful at resolving current problems in management.
   C. There is a common conviction of manages that their goals are difficult to achieve.
   D. Managers are far more concerned about correcting today's problems than with preventing tomorrow's.

   5.____

6. Which of the following should generally have the MOST influence on the selection of supervisors?
   A. Experience within the work unit where the vacancies exist
   B. Amount of money needed to effect the promotion
   C. Personal preferences of the administration
   D. Evaluation of capacity to exercise supervisory responsibilities

7. In questioning a potential administrator for selection purposes, the one of the following practices which is MOST desirable is to
   A. encourage the job applicant to give primarily *yes* or *no* replies
   B. get the applicant to talk freely and in detail about his background
   C. let the job applicant speak most of the time
   D. probe the applicant's attitudes, motivation, and willingness to accept responsibility

8. In implementing the managerial function of training subordinates, it is USEFUL to know that a widely agreed-upon definition of human learning is that learning
   A. is a relatively permanent change in behavior that results from reinforced practice or experience
   B. involves an improvement, but not necessarily a change in behavior
   C. involves a change in behavior, but not necessarily an improvement
   D. is a temporary change in behavior which must be subject to practice or experience

9. If a manager were thinking about using a committee of subordinates to solve an operating problem, which of the following would generally NOT be an advantage of such use of the committee approach?
   A. Improved coordination   B. Low cost
   C. Increased motivation   D. Integrated judgment

10. Which one of the following management approaches MOST often uses model-building techniques to solve management problems?
    _____ approach.
    A. Behavioral   B. Fiscal   C. Quantitative   D. Process

11. Of the following, the MOST serious risk in using budgets as a tool for management control is the
    A. probable neglect of other good management practices
    B. likelihood of guesswork because of the need to plan far in advance
    C. possibility of undue emphasis on factors that are easiest to measure
    D. danger of making qualitative rather than quantitative assessments of performance

12. In government budgeting, the problem of relating financial transactions to the fiscal year in which they are budgeted is BEST met by
    A. determining the cash balance by comparing how much money has been received and how much has been paid out
    B. applying net revenue to the fiscal year in which they are collected as offset by relevant expenses

C. adopting a system whereby appropriations are entered when they are received and expenditures are entered when they are paid out
D. entering expenditures on the books when the obligation to make the expenditure is made

13. If the agency's bookkeeping system records income when it is received and expenditures when the money is paid out this system is USUALLY known as a _____ system.
    A. cash
    B. flow-payment
    C. deferred
    D. fiscal year income

14. An audit, as the term applies to budget execution, is MOST NEARLY a
    A. procedure based on the budget estimates
    B. control exercised by the executive on the legislature in the establishment of program priorities
    C. check on the legality of expenditures and is based on the appropriations act
    D. requirement which must be met before funds can be spent

15. In government budgeting, there is a procedure known as *allotment*.
    Of the following statements which relate to allotment, select the one that is MOST generally considered to be correct.
    Allotment
    A. increases the practice of budget units coming back to the legislature branch for supplemental appropriations
    B. is simply an example of red tape
    C. eliminates the requirement of timing of expenditures
    D. is designed to prevent waste

16. In government budgeting, the establishment of the schedules of allotments is MOST generally the responsibility of the
    A. budget unit and the legislature
    B. budget unit and the executive
    C. budget unit only
    D. executive and the legislature

17. Of the following statements relating to preparation of an organization's budget request, which is the MOST generally valid precaution?
    A. Give specific instructions on the format or budget requests and required supporting data
    B. Because of the complexity of preparing a budget request, avoid argumentation to support the requests
    C. Put requests in whatever format is desirable
    D. Consider that final approval will be given to initial estimates

18. Of the following statements which relate to the budget process in a well-organized government, select the one that is MOST NEARLY correct.
    A. The budget cycle is the step-by-step process which is repeated each and every fiscal year.
    B. Securing approval of the budget does not take place within the budget cycle.

C. The development of a new budget and putting it into effect is a two-step process known as the budget cycle.
D. The fiscal period, usually a fiscal year, has no relation to the budget cycle.

19. If a manager were asked what PPBS stands for, he would be RIGHT if he said _____ budgeting system.
    A. public planning
    B. planning programming
    C. planning projections
    D. programming procedures

Questions 20-21.

DIRECTIONS: Questions 20 and 21 are to be answered on the basis of the following information.

Sample Budget

Refuse Collection	Amount
Personal Services	$30,000
Contractual Services	5,000
Supplies and Materials	5,000
Capital Outlay	10,000
	$50,000

Residential Collections	
Dwellings – 1 pickup per week	1,000
Tons of refuse collected per year	375
Cost of collections per ton	$ 8
Cost per dwelling pickup per year	$ 3
Total annual cost	$3,000

20. The sample budget shown is a simplified example of a _____ budget.
    A. factorial   B. performance   C. qualitative   D. rational

21. The budget shown in the sample differs CHIEFLY from line-item and program budgets in that it includes
    A. objects of expenditure but not activities or functions
    B. only activities, functions, and control
    C. activities and functions but not objects of expenditures
    D. levels of service

Question 22.

DIRECTIONS: Question 22 is to be answered on the basis of the following information.

Sample Budget

Environmental Safety
  Air Pollution Protection
    Personal Services $20,000,000
    Contractual Services   4,000,000
    Supplies and Materials   4,000,000
    Capital Outlay   2,000,000
      Total Air Pollution Protection $30,000,000

  Water Pollution Protection
    Personal Services $23,000,000
    Supplies and Materials   4,500,000
    Capital Outlay   20,500,000
      Total Water Pollution Protection $48,000,000

Total Environmental Safety $78,000,000

22. Based on the above budget, which is the MOST valid statement?
    A. Environmental Safety, Air Pollution Protection, and Water Pollution Protection could all be considered program elements.
    B. The object listings included water pollution protection and capital outlay.
    C. Examples of the program element listings in the above are personal services and supplies and materials
    D. Contractual Services and Environmental Safety were the program element listings.

23. Which of the following is NOT an advantage of a program budget over a line-item budget?
    A program budget
    A. allows us to set up priority lists in deciding what activities we will spend our money on
    B. gives us more control over expenditures than a line-item budget
    C. is more informative in that we know the broad purposes of spending money
    D. enables us to see if one program is getting much less money than the others

24. If a manager were trying to explain the fundamental difference between traditional accounting theory and practice and the newer practice of managerial accounting, he would be MOST accurate if he said that
    A. traditional accounting practice focused on providing information for persons outside organizations, while managerial accounting focuses on providing information for people inside organizations
    B. traditional accounting practice focused on providing information for persons inside organizations while managerial accounting focuses on providing information for persons outside organizations

6 (#2)

C. managerial accounting is exclusively concerned with historical facts while traditional accounting stresses future projections exclusively
D. traditional accounting practice is more budget-focused than managerial accounting

25. Which of the following formulas is used to determine the number of days required to process work?
_____ = Days to Process Work

A. $\dfrac{\text{Employees} \times \text{Daily Output}}{\text{Volume}}$

B. $\dfrac{\text{Volume} \times \text{Daily Output}}{\text{Volume}}$

C. $\dfrac{\text{Volume}}{\text{Employees} \times \text{Daily Output}}$

D. $\dfrac{\text{Employees} \times \text{Volume}}{\text{Daily Output}}$

25.____

KEY (CORRECT ANSWERS)

1.	C	11.	C
2.	C	12.	D
3.	D	13.	A
4.	B	14.	C
5.	D	15.	D
6.	D	16.	C
7.	D	17.	A
8.	A	18.	A
9.	B	19.	B
10.	C	20.	B

21. D
22. A
23. B
24. A
25. C

TEST 3

DIRECTIONS: Each question or incomplete statement is followed by several suggested answers or completions. Select the one that BEST answers the question or completes the statement. *PRINT THE LETTER OF THE CORRECT ANSWER IN THE SPACE AT THE RIGHT.*

1. Electronic data processing equipment can produce more information faster than can be generated by any other means.
   In view of this, the MOST important problem faced by management at present is to
   A. keep computers fully occupied
   B. find enough computer personnel
   C. assimilate and properly evaluate the information
   D. obtain funds to establish appropriate information systems

   1.____

2. A well-designed management information system ESSENTIALLY provides each executive and manager the information he needs for
   A. determining computer time requirements
   B. planning and measuring results
   C. drawing a new organization chart
   D. developing a new office layout

   2.____

3. It is generally agreed that management policies should be periodically reappraised and restated in accordance with current conditions.
   Of the following, the approach which would be MOST effective in determining whether a policy should be revised is to
   A. conduct interviews with staff members at all levels in order to ascertain the relationship between the policy and actual practice
   B. make proposed revisions in the policy and apply it to current problems
   C. make up hypothetical situations using both the old policy and a revised version in order to make comparisons
   D. call a meeting of top level staff in order to discuss ways of revising the policy

   3.____

4. Every manager has many occasions to lead a conference or participate in a conference of some sort.
   Of the following statements that pertain to conferences and conference leadership, which is generally considered to be MOST valid?
   A. Since World War II, the trend has been toward fewer shared decisions and more conferences.
   B. The most important part of a conference leader's job is to direct discussion.
   C. In providing opportunities for group interaction, management should avoid consideration of its past management philosophy.
   D. A good administrator cannot lead a good conference if he is a poor public speaker.

   4.____

5. Of the following, it is usually LEAST desirable for a conference leader to
   A. turn the question to the person who asked it
   B. summarize proceedings periodically
   C. make a practice of not repeating questions
   D. ask a question without indicating who is to reply

6. The behavioral school of management thought bases its beliefs on certain assumptions.
   Which of the following is NOT a belief of this school of thought?
   A. People tend to seek and accept responsibility.
   B. Most people can be creative in solving problems.
   C. People prefer security above all else.
   D. Commitment is the most important factor in motivating people.

7. The one of the following objectives which would be LEAST appropriate as a major goal of research in the field of human resources management is to
   A. predict future conditions, events, and manpower needs
   B. evaluate established policies, programs, and practices
   C. evaluate proposed policies, programs, and practices
   D. identify deficient organizational units and apply suitable penalties

8. Of the following general interviewing methods or techniques, the one that is USUALLY considered to be effective in counseling, grievances, and appraisal interviews is the _____ interview.
   A. directed   B. non-directed   C. panel   D. patterned

9. The ESSENTIAL first phase of decision-making is
   A. finding alternative solutions
   B. making a diagnosis of the problem
   C. selecting the plan to follow
   D. analyzing and comparing alternative solutions

10. Assume that, in a certain organization, a situation has developed in which there is little difference in status or authority between individuals.
    Which of the following would be the MOST likely result with regard to communication in this organization?
    A. Both the accuracy and flow of communication will be improved.
    B. Both the accuracy and flow of communication will substantially decrease.
    C. Employees will seek more formal lines of communication.
    D. Neither the flow nor the accuracy of communication will be improved over the former hierarchical structure.

11. The main function of many agency administrative offices is *information management*. Information that is received by an administrative officer may be classified as active or passive, depending upon whether or not it requires the recipient to take some action.

Of the following, the item received which is clearly the MOST active information is
- A. an appointment of a new staff member
- B. a payment voucher for a new desk
- C. a press release concerning a past city event
- D. the minutes of a staff meeting

12. Which one of the following sets BEST describes the general order in which to teach an operation to a new employee?
    - A. Prepare, present, tryout, follow-up
    - B. Prepare, test, tryout, re-test
    - C. Present, test, tryout, follow-up
    - D. Test, present, follow-up, re-test

13. Of the following, public employees may be separated from public service
    - A. for the same reasons which are generally acceptable for discharging employees in private industry
    - B. only under the most trying circumstances
    - C. under procedures that are neither formalized nor subject to review
    - D. solely in extreme cases involving offenses of gravest character

14. Of the following, the one LEAST considered to be a communication barrier is
    - A. group feedback
    - B. charged words
    - C. selective perception
    - D. symbolic meanings

15. Of the following ways for a manager to handle his appointments, the BEST way, according to experts in administration, generally is to
    - A. schedule his own appointments and inform his secretary not to reserve his time without his approval
    - B. encourage everyone to make appointments through his secretary and tell her when he makes his own appointments
    - C. see no one who has not made a previous appointment
    - D. permit anyone to see him without an appointment

16. Assume that a manager decides to examine closely one of five units under his supervision to uncover problems common to all five.
    His research technique is MOST closely related to the method called
    - A. experimentation
    - B. simulation
    - C. linear analysis
    - D. sampling

17. If one views the process of management as a dynamic process, which one of the following functions is NOT a legitimate part of that process?
    - A. Communication
    - B. Decision-making
    - C. Organizational slack
    - D. Motivation

18. Which of the following would be the BEST statement of a budget-oriented purpose for a government administrator? To
    A. provide 200 hours of instruction in basic reading for 3,500 adult illiterates at a cost of $1 million in the next fiscal year
    B. inform the public of adult educational programs
    C. facilitate the transfer to a city agency of certain functions of a federally-funded program which is being phased out
    D. improve the reading skills of the adult citizens in the city

19. Modern management philosophy and practices are changing to accommodate the expectations and motivations of organization personnel.
    Which of the following terms INCORRECTLY describes these newer managerial approaches?
    A. Rational management
    B. Participative management
    C. Decentralization
    D. Democratic supervision

20. Management studies support the hypothesis that, in spite of the tendency of employees to censor the information communicated to their supervisor, subordinates are MORE likely to communicate problem-oriented information upward when they have
    A. a long period of service in the organization
    B. a high degree of trust in the supervisor
    C. a high educational level
    D. low status on the organizational ladder

KEY (CORRECT ANSWERS)

1.	C	11.	A
2.	B	12.	A
3.	A	13.	A
4.	B	14.	A
5.	A	15.	B
6.	C	16.	D
7.	D	17.	C
8.	B	18.	A
9.	B	19.	A
10.	D	20.	B

WORK SCHEDULING

EXAMINATION SECTION
TEST 1

DIRECTIONS: Each question or incomplete statement is followed by several suggested answers or completions. Select the one that BEST answers the question or completes the statement. *PRINT THE LETTER OF THE CORRECT ANSWER IN THE SPACE AT THE RIGHT.*

Questions 1-6.

DIRECTIONS: Questions 1 through 6 are to be answered SOLELY on the basis of the information given in the ELEVATOR OPERATORS' WORK SCHEDULE shown below.

ELEVATOR OPERATORS' WORK SCHEDULE				
Operator	Hours of Work	A.M. Relief Period	Lunch Hour	P.M. Relief Period
Anderson	8:30-4:30	10:20-10:30	12:00-1:00	2:20-2:30
Carter	8:00-4:00	10:10-10:20	11:45-12:45	2:30-2:40
Daniels	9:00-5:00	10:20-10:30	12:30-1:30	3:15-3:25
Grand	9:30-5:30	11:30-11:40	1:00-2:00	4:05-4:15
Jones	7:45-3:45	9:45-9:55	11:30-12:30	2:05-2:15
Lewis	9:45-5:45	11:40-11:50	1:15-2:15	4:20-4:30
Nance	8:45-4:45	10:50-11:00	12:30-1:30	3:05-3:15
Perkins	8:00-4:00	10:00-10:10	12:00-1:00	2:40-2:50
Russo	7:45-3:45	9:30-9:40	11:30-12:30	2:10-2:20
Smith	9:45-5:45	11:45-11:55	1:15-2:15	4:05-4:15

1. The two operators who are on P.M. relief at the SAME time are

   A. Anderson and Daniels B. Carter and Perkins
   C. Jones and Russo D. Grand and Smith

   1._____

2. Of the following, the two operators who have the SAME lunch hour are

   A. Anderson and Perkins B. Daniels and Russo
   C. Grand and Smith D. Nance and Russo

   2._____

3. At 12:15, the number of operators on their lunch hour is

   A. 3 B. 4 C. 5 D. 6

   3._____

4. The operator who has an A.M. relief period right after Perkins and a P.M. relief period right before Perkins is

   A. Russo B. Nance C. Daniels D. Carter

   4._____

5. The number of operators who are scheduled to be working at 4:40 is

   A. 5 B. 6 C. 7 D. 8

   5._____

6. According to the schedule, it is MOST correct to say that
    A. no operator has a relief period during the time that another operator has a lunch hour
    B. each operator has to wait an identical amount of time between the end of lunch and the beginning of P.M. relief period
    C. no operator has a relief period before 9:45 or after 4:00
    D. each operator is allowed a total of 1 hour and 20 minutes for lunch hour and relief periods

---

KEY (CORRECT ANSWERS)

1. D
2. A
3. C
4. D
5. A
6. D

TEST 2

DIRECTIONS: Each question or incomplete statement is followed by several suggested answers or completions. Select the one that BEST answers the question or completes the statement. *PRINT THE LETTER OF THE CORRECT ANSWER IN THE SPACE AT THE RIGHT.*

Questions 1-7.

DIRECTIONS: Questions 1 through 7 are to be answered SOLELY on the basis of the time sheet and instructions given below.

The following time sheet indicates the times that seven laundry workers arrived and left each day for the week of August 23. The times they arrived for work are shown under the heading IN, and the times they left are shown under the heading OUT. The letter (P) indicates time which was used for personal business. Time used for this purpose is charged to annual leave. Lunch time is one-half hour from noon to 12:30 P.M. and is not accounted for on this time record.

The employees on this shift are scheduled to work from 8:00 A.M. to 4:00 P.M. Lateness is charged to annual leave. Reporting after 8:00 A.M. is considered late.

	MON.		TUES.		WED.		THURS.		FRI.	
	AM IN	PM OUT	AM IN	PM OUT	AM IN	PM OUT	AM IN	PM OUT	AM IN	PM OUT
Baxter	7:50	4:01	7:49	4:07	8:00	4:07	8:20	4:00	7:42	4:03
Gardner	8:02	4:00	8:20	4:00	8:05	3:30(P)	8:00	4:03	8:00	4:07
Clements	8:00	4:04	8:03	4:01	7:59	4:00	7:54	4:06	7:59	4:00
Tompkins	7:56	4:00	Annual leave		8:00	4:07	7:59	4:00	8:00	4:01
Wagner	8:04	4:03	7:40	4:00	7:53	4:04	8:00	4:09	7:53	4:00
Patterson	8:00	2:30(P)	8:15	4:04	Sick leave		7:45	4:00	7:59	4:04
Cunningham	7:43	4:02	7:50	4:00	7:59	4:02	8:00	4:10	8:00	4:00

1. Which one of the following laundry workers did NOT have any time charged to annual leave or sick leave during the week? 1._____

    A. Gardner   B. Clements   C. Tompkins   D. Cunningham

2. On which day did ALL the laundry workers arrive on time? 2._____

    A. Monday   B. Wednesday   C. Thursday   D. Friday

3. Which of the following laundry workers used time to take care of personal business? 3._____

    A. Baxter and Clements
    C. Gardner and Patterson
    B. Patterson and Cunningham
    D. Wagner and Tompkins

4. How many laundry workers were late on Monday? 4._____

    A. 1   B. 2   C. 3   D. 4

5. Which one of the following laundry workers arrived late on three of the five days? 5._____

    A. Baxter   B. Gardner   C. Wagner   D. Patterson

6. The percentage of laundry workers reporting to work late on Tuesday is MOST NEARLY 6._____

   A. 15%   B. 25%   C. 45%   D. 50%

7. The percentage of laundry workers that were absent for an entire day during the week is MOST NEARLY 7._____

   A. 6%   B. 9%   C. 15%   D. 30%

KEY (CORRECT ANSWERS)

1. D
2. D
3. C
4. B
5. B
6. C
7. D

TEST 3

Questions 1-9.

DIRECTIONS: Questions 1 through 9 are to be answered SOLELY on the basis of the following information and timesheet given below.

The following is a foreman's timesheet for his crew for one week. The hours worked each day or the reason the man was off on that day are shown on the sheet. *R* means rest day. *A* means annual leave. *S* means sick leave. Where a man worked only part of a day, both the number of hours worked and the number of hours taken off are entered. The reason for absence is entered in parentheses next to the number of hours taken off.

Name	Saturday	Sunday	Monday	Tuesday	Wednesday	Thursday	Friday
Smith	R	R	7	7	7	3 4(A)	7
Jones	R	7	7	7	7	7	R
Green	R	R	7	7	S	S	S
White	R	R	7	7	A	7	7
Doe	7	7	7	7	7	R	R
Brown	R	R	A	7	7	7	7
Black	R	R	S	7	7	7	7
Reed	R	R	7	7	7	7	S
Roe	R	R	A	7	7	7	7
Lane	7	R	R	7	7	A	S

1. The caretaker who worked EXACTLY 21 hours during the week is

   A. Lane   B. Roe   C. Smith   D. White

2. The TOTAL number of hours worked by all caretakers during the week is

   A. 268   B. 276   C. 280   D. 288

3. The two days of the week on which MOST caretakers were off are

   A. Thursday and Friday   B. Friday and Saturday
   C. Saturday and Sunday   D. Sunday and Monday

4. The day on which three caretakers were off on sick leave is

   A. Monday   B. Friday   C. Saturday   D. Sunday

5. The two workers who took LEAST time off during the week are

   A. Doe and Reed   B. Jones and Doe
   C. Reed and Smith   D. Smith and Jones

6. The caretaker who worked the LEAST number of hours during the week is

   A. Brown   B. Green   C. Lane   D. Roe

7. The caretakers who did NOT work on Thursday are

   A. Doe, White, and Smith
   B. Green, Doe, and Lane
   C. Green, Doe, and Smith
   D. Green, Lane, and Smith

8. The day on which one caretaker worked ONLY 3 hours is 8.____
   A. Friday   B. Saturday   C. Thursday   D. Wednesday

9. The day on which ALL caretakers worked is 9.____
   A. Monday   B. Thursday   C. Tuesday   D. Wednesday

KEY (CORRECT ANSWERS)

1. A
2. B
3. C
4. B
5. B

6. B
7. B
8. C
9. C

TEST 4

Questions 1-6.

DIRECTIONS: Questions 1 through 6 are to be answered SOLELY on the basis of the table below which shows the initial requests made by staff for vacation. It is to be used with the RULES AND GUIDELINES to make the decisions and judgments called for in each of the questions.

VACATION REQUESTS FOR THE ONE YEAR PERIOD FROM MAY 1, YEAR X THROUGH APRIL 30, YEAR Y				
Name	Work Assignment	Date Appointed	Accumulated Annual Leave Days	Vacation Periods Requested
DeMarco	MVO	Mar. 2003	25	May 3-21; Oct. 25-Nov. 5
Moore	Dispatcher	Dec. 1997	32	May 24-June 4; July 12-16
Kingston	MVO	Apr. 2007	28	May 24-June 11; Feb. 7-25
Green	MVO	June 2006	26	June 7-18; Sept. 6-24
Robinson	MVO	July 2008	30	June 28-July 9; Nov. 15-26
Reilly	MVO	Oct. 2009	23	July 5-9; Jan. 31-Mar. 3
Stevens	MVO	Sept. 1996	31	July 5-23; Oct. 4-29
Costello	MVO	Sept. 1998	31	July 5-30; Oct. 4-22
Maloney	Dispatcher	Aug. 1992	35	July 5-Aug. 6; Nov. 1-5
Hughes	Director	Feb. 1990	38	July 26-Sept. 3
Lord	MVO	Jan. 2010	20	Aug. 9-27; Feb. 7-25
Diaz	MVO	Dec. 2009	28	Aug. 9-Sept. 10
Krimsky	MVO	May 2006	22	Oct. 18-22: Nov. 22-Dec. 10

RULES AND GUIDELINES

1. The two Dispatchers cannot be on vacation at the same time, nor can a Dispatcher be on vacation at the same time as the Director.

2. For the period June 1 through September 30, not more than three MVO's can be on vacation at the same time.

3. For the period October 1 through May 31, not more than two MVO's at a time can be on vacation.

4. In cases where the same vacation time is requested by too many employees for all of them to be given the time under the rules, the requests of those who have worked the longest will be granted.

5. No employee may take more leave days than the number of annual leave days accumulated and shown in the table.

6. All vacation periods shown in the table and described in the questions below begin on a Monday and end on a Friday.

7. Employees work a five-day week (Monday through Friday). They are off weekends and holidays with no charges to leave balances. When a holiday falls on a Saturday or Sunday, employees are given the following Monday off without charge to annual leave.

8. Holidays:

May 31	October 25	January 1
July 4	November 2	February 12
September 6	November 25	February 21
October 11	December 25	February 21

9. An employee shall be given any part of his initial requests that is permissible under the above rules and shall have first right to it despite any further adjustment of schedule.

---

1. Until adjustments in the vacation schedule can be made, the vacation dates that can be approved for Krimsky are

   A. Oct. 18-22; Nov. 22-Dec. 10
   B. Oct. 18-22; Nov. 29-Dec. 10
   C. Oct. 18-22 *only*
   D. Nov. 22-Dec. 10 *only*

2. Until adjustments in the vacation schedule can be made, the vacation dates that can be approved for Maloney are

   A. July 5-Aug. 6; Nov. 1-5
   B. July 5-23; Nov. 1-5
   C. July 5-9; Nov. 1-5
   D. Nov. 1-5 *only*

3. According to the table, Lord wants a vacation in August and another in February. Until adjustments in the vacation schedule can be made, he can be allowed to take _____ of the August vacation and _____ of the February vacation.

   A. all; none
   B. all; almost half
   C. almost all; almost half
   D. almost half; all

4. Costello cannot be given all the vacation he has requested because

   A. the MVO's who have more seniority than he has have requested time he wishes
   B. he does not have enough accumulated annual leave
   C. a dispatcher is applying for vacation at the same time as Costello
   D. there are five people who want vacation in July

5. According to the table, how many leave days will DeMarco be charged for his vacation from October 25 through November 5?

   A. 10   B. 9   C. 8   D. 7

6. How many leave days will Moore use if he uses the requested vacation allowable to him under the rules?

   A. 9   B. 10   C. 14   D. 15

KEY (CORRECT ANSWERS)

1. D
2. B
3. A
4. B
5. C
6. A

TEST 5

Questions 1-8.

DIRECTIONS: Questions 1 through 8 are to be answered SOLELY on the basis of Charts I, II, III, and IV. Assume that you are the supervisor of Operators R, S, T, U, V, W, and X, and it is your responsibility to schedule their lunch hours.

The charts each represent a possible scheduling of lunch hours during a lunch period from 11:30 - 2:00. An operator-hour is one hour of time spent by one operator. Each box on the chart represents one half-hour. The boxes marked L represent the time when each operator is scheduled to have her lunch hour. For example, in Chart I, next to Operator R, the boxes for 11:30 - 12:00 and 12:00 -12:30 are marked L. This means that Operator R is scheduled to have her lunch hour from 11:30 to 12:30.

I

	11:30-12:00	12:00-12:30	12:30-1:00	1:00-1:30	1:30-2:00
R	L	L			
S		L	L		
T		L	L		
U			L	L	
V			L	L	
W				L	L
X				L	L

II

	11:30-12:00	12:00-12:30	12:30-1:00	1:00-1:30	1:30-2:00
R				L	L
S		L	L		
T	L	L			
U		L	L		
V				L	L
W				L	L
X	L	L			

III

	11:30-12:00	12:00-12:30	12:30-1:00	1:00-1:30	1:30-2:00
R	L	L			
S				L	L
T	L	L			
U			L	L	
V	L	L			
W			L	L	
X			L	L	

IV

	11:30-12:00	12:00-12:30	12:30-1:00	1:00-1:30	1:30-2:00
R	L	L			
S	L	L			
T		L	L		
U			L	L	
V				L	L
W				L	L
X				L	L

1. If, under the schedule represented in Chart II, Operator R has her lunch hour changed to 12:30-1:30, that leaves how many operator-hours of phone coverage from 1:00-2:00?

   A. 2   B. 2 1/2   C. 3   D. 4 1/2

2. If Operator S asks you whether she and Operator T may have the same lunch hour, you could accommodate her by using the schedule in Chart

   A. I   B. II   C. III   D. IV

3. From past experience you know that the part of the lunch period when the phones are busiest is from 12:30-1:30. Which chart shows the BEST phone coverage from 12:30 to 1:30?

   A. I   B. II   C. III   D. IV

4. At least three operators have the same lunch hour according to Chart(s)

   A. II and III
   B. II and IV
   C. III only
   D. IV only

5. Which chart would provide the POOREST phone coverage during the period 12:00-1:30, based on total number of operator-hours from 12:00 to 1:30?

   A. I   B. II   C. III   D. IV

6. Which chart would make it possible for U, W, and X to have the same lunch hour?

   A. I   B. II   C. III   D. IV

7. The portion of the lunch period during which the telephones are least busy is 11:30-12:30.
   Which chart is MOST likely to have been designed with that fact in mind?

   A. I   B. II   C. III   D. IV

8. Assume that you have decided to use Chart IV to schedule your operators' lunch hours on a specific day. Operator T asks you if she can have her lunch hour changed to 1:00-2:00.
   If you grant her request, how many operators will be working during the period 12:00 to 12:30?

   A. 1   B. 2   C. 4   D. 5

KEY (CORRECT ANSWERS)

1. D
2. A
3. B
4. A
5. A

6. C
7. C
8. D

TEST 6

Questions 1-13.

DIRECTIONS: Questions 1 through 13 consist of a statement. You are to indicate whether the statement is TRUE (T) or FALSE (F). *PRINT THE LETTER OF THE CORRECT ANSWER IN THE SPACE AT THE RIGHT.* Questions 1 through 13 are to be answered SOLELY on the basis of the information given in the table below.

DEPARTMENT OF FERRIES
ATTENDANTS WORK ASSIGNMENT - JULY 2003

Name	Year Employed	Ferry Assigned	Hours of Work	Lunch Period	Days Off
Adams	1999	Hudson	7 AM - 3 PM	11-12	Fri. and Sat.
Baker	1992	Monroe	7 AM - 3 PM	11-12	Sun. and Mon.
Gunn	1995	Troy	8 AM - 4 PM	12-1	Fri. and Sat.
Hahn	1989	Erie	9 AM - 5 PM	1-2	Sat. and Sun.
King	1998	Albany	7 AM - 3 PM	11-12	Sun. and Mon.
Nash	1993	Hudson	11 AM - 7 PM	3-4	Sun. and Mon.
Olive	2003	Fulton	10 AM - 6 PM	2-3	Sat. and Sun.
Queen	2002	Albany	11 AM - 7 PM	3-4	Fri. and Sat.
Rose	1990	Troy	11 AM - 7 PM	3-4	Sun. and Mon.
Smith	1991	Monroe	10 AM - 6 PM	2-3	Fri. and Sat.

1. The chart shows that there are only five (5) ferries being used.   1.____

2. The attendant who has been working the LONGEST time is Rose.   2.____

3. The <u>Troy</u> has one more attendant assigned to it than the Erie.   3.____

4. Two (2) attendants are assigned to work from 10 P.M. to 6 A.M.   4.____

5. According to the chart, no more than one attendant was hired in any year.   5.____

6. The NEWEST employee is Olive.   6.____

7. There are as many attendants on the 7 to 3 shift as on the 11 to 7 shift.   7.____

8. MOST of the attendants have their lunch either between 12 and 1 or 2 and 3.   8.____

9. All the employees work four (4) hours before they go to lunch.   9.____

10. On the <u>Hudson</u>, Adams goes to lunch when Nash reports to work.   10.____

11. All the attendants who work on the 7 to 3 shift are off on Saturday and Sunday.   11.____

12. All the attendants have either a Saturday or Sunday as one of their days off.   12.____

13. At least two (2) attendants are assigned to each ferry.   13.____

KEY (CORRECT ANSWERS)

1. F	6. T	11. F
2. F	7. T	12. T
3. T	8. F	13. F
4. F	9. T	
5. T	10. T	

EXAMINATION SECTION
TEST 1

DIRECTIONS: Each question or incomplete statement is followed by several suggested answers or completions. Select the one that BEST answers the question or completes the statement. *PRINT THE LETTER OF THE CORRECT ANSWER IN THE SPACE AT THE RIGHT.*

1. Assume that a supervisor finds that his employees have become fatigued from doing a very long and repetitive job.
   The one of the following which would be the BEST way to relieve this fatigue is to
   A. assign other work so that the employees can switch to different assignments in the middle of the day
   B. let the employees listen to a radio while they work
   C. break the job down into very small parts so that each employee can concentrate on one simple task
   D. allow the employees to take frequent rest periods

   1.____

2. Assume that one of your subordinates is injured and will be out for at least six weeks.
   Of the following, the BEST way to handle the work normally assigned to this person is to
   A. allow the work to remain uncompleted until the injured person returns, since he is the one who can BEST do this work
   B. divide this work equally among the persons under your supervision who can do this work
   C. do all the work yourself
   D. give the injured person's work to the most efficient member of your staff

   2.____

3. Suppose that another supervisor tells you about a new way to organize some of your unit's work. The idea sounds good to you. However, before you were in this unit, a similar plan was tried and it failed.
   The MOST important thing for you to do FIRST is to
   A. find out why the previous attempt failed
   B. suggest that the other supervisor tell his idea to top management
   C. try the plan to see whether it works
   D. find proof that the plan has worked elsewhere

   3.____

4. One of your subordinates comes to you with a grievance. You discuss it with him so that you may fully understand the problem as he sees it. However, since you are uncertain as to the proper answer, you should
   A. tell him that you cannot help him with this problem
   B. tell him that you will have to check further and make an appointment to see him again
   C. send him to see your immediate superior for a solution to the problem
   D. ask him to find out from his co-workers whether this problem has come up before

   4.____

5. A supervisor reprimanded one of his subordinates severely for making a serious error in judgment while performing an assignment for which he had volunteered.
The supervisor's action was
   A. *incorrect*, chiefly because in the future the worker will probably try to avoid taking on responsibility
   B. *correct*, chiefly because this will insure that the worker will not make the same mistake in the future
   C. *correct*, chiefly because the worker should be discouraged from using his own judgment on the job
   D. *incorrect*, chiefly because the reprimand came too late to correct the error that had already been made

6. Of the following, the BEST way for a supervisor to inform all his subordinates of a change in lunch rules is, in MOST cases, to
   A. call a staff meeting
   B. tell each one individually
   C. issue a memorandum
   D. tell one or two employees to pass the word around

7. For a supervisor to assign work giving only general instructions to his subordinate would be advisable when
   A. the supervisor is confident that the worker knows how to do the job
   B. the assignment is a simple one
   C. the subordinate is himself a supervisory employee
   D. errors in the work will not cause serious delay

8. One of the DISADVANTAGES of setting minimum standards of performance for custodial employees is that
   A. such standards eliminate the basis for evaluating employees
   B. the custodial employees may keep their performance at the minimum level
   C. standards are always subject to change
   D. the supervisor may feel that his initiative is being restricted

9. One of your subordinates has been functioning below his usual level. You feel that something of a personal nature may be affecting his work. When you ask him casually whether anything is wrong, he says everything is fine.
As a next step, it would be BEST to
   A. make frequent casual and humorous comments about the poor quality of his work but refrain, at this time, from any serious discussion
   B. warn him that failure to maintain his customary level of performance might result in disciplinary action
   C. express your concern privately and reveal your interest in the reason for his change in work performance
   D. discuss with him the work of another employee, suggesting that the other employee would be a good example to follow

10. Assume you are teaching a new job to one of your subordinates. After you have demonstrated the job, you can BEST maintain the worker's interest by
    A. showing him training films about the job
    B. giving him printed material that explains why the job is important
    C. having him observe other workers do the job
    D. letting him attempt to do the job by himself under supervision

11. *Insubordination is sometimes a protest against inferior or arbitrary leadership.*
    For the supervisor, the MOST basic implication of the above statement is:
    A. Accusations of insubordination are easy to make, but usually difficult to prove.
    B. Insubordination cannot be permitted if an organization wishes to remain effective.
    C. When an employee discusses an order instead of carrying it out, he has not understood it.
    D. When an employee questions an order, review it to make sure it is reasonable.

12. In appraising a subordinate's mistakes, a supervisor should ALWAYS consider the
    A. absolute number of mistakes, without regard to severity
    B. number of mistakes in proportion to the number of decisions made
    C. total number of mistakes made by other, regardless of assignment
    D. number of mistakes which were discovered upon higher review

13. If you are the supervisor of an office in which the work frequently involves lifting heavy boxes, you should instruct your staff in the proper method of lifting to avoid injury.
    In giving these instructions, you should stress that a person lifting heavy objects MUST
    A. keep his feet close together
    B. bend at the waist
    C. keep his back as straight as possible
    D. use his back muscles to straighten up

14. Of the following, the BEST qualified supervisor is one who
    A. knows the basic principles and procedures of all the jobs which he supervises
    B. has detailed working knowledge of all aspects of the job he supervises but knows little about principles of supervision
    C. is able to do exceptionally well at least one of the jobs which he supervises and as some knowledge of the others
    D. knows little or nothing about most of the jobs which he supervises but knows the principles of supervision

15. The rate at which an employee will learn will vary according to a number of considerations.
    Of the following, which is LEAST likely to be controllable by the supervisor or the trainer? The
    A. manner in which the material is presented
    B. state of readiness of the learner
    C. scheduling of practice sessions
    D. nature of the material

16. When considering whether to use written material rather than oral instructions as a means of giving instructions to employees, the one of the following which should be given GREATEST consideration is the employees'
    A. personal preferences
    B. attitude toward supervision
    C. general educational level
    D. salary level

17. Assume that one of your subordinates has been assigned to attend job training classes.
    The one of the following which would probably be the BEST evidence of the success of the course is that the employee
    A. feels that he has learned something
    B. continues to study after the course is over
    C. has had a good class record
    D. improves in his work performance

18. Of the following, the situation LEAST likely to result if a supervisor shows favoritism toward particular employees is
    A. laxity in the work of the favored employees
    B. resentment from the other, less-favored employees
    C. increased ability among the favored employees
    D. lowering of morale among employees

19. The one of the following reasons for evaluating employees' performance, whether done formally or informally, which is NOT considered to be POSITIVE in nature is to
    A. give individual counsel to employees
    B. motivate employees toward improvement
    C. provide recognition of superior service
    D. set penalties for substandard performance

20. Assume that, because there has been an unexpected and temporary increase in the short-term work of your unit, you have had temporarily assigned to you several staff members from another agency.
    Of the following, in dealing with these employees, it would be LEAST advisable to
    A. assign them to long-term projects
    B. organize tasks so that they can begin work immediately
    C. set standards, making allowances to give them time to learn your ways
    D. direct them in the same way, in general, as you do your regular staff

21. It has been suggested that one way to increase employee productivity would be to require employees dealing with the public to have proficiency in a relevant foreign language.
    Of the following, the MAJOR reason for implementing such a proposal, from the viewpoint of effective public administration, would be to
    A. encourage the foreign-born to learn English
    B. exchange information more rapidly and accurately
    C. increase the public prestige of the agency
    D. stimulate ethnic pride among all groups

22. Assume that the clerk who normally keeps your unit's records will be on vacation for four weeks.
    If other clerks are equally qualified to keep these records, your BEST choice to replace the clerk would be the person who
    A. has skills which are needed least for other duties during this period
    B. volunteers for this work
    C. is next in turn for a special assignment
    D. has handled this task before

23. Assume that you have under your supervision several young clerical employees who have the bad habit of fooling around when they should be working.
    Of the following, the BEST disciplinary action to take would be to
    A. ignore it; these young people will outgrow it
    B. join in the fun briefly in order to bring it to a quicker end each time it occurs
    C. bring to their attention the fact that this behavior is not acceptable and if it continues shift the make-up of the group to keep these young persons apart
    D. warn them that this type of behavior is reason for dismissal and be quick to make an example of the first one who starts it again

24. Seeking the advice of community leaders has human relations value for a public agency in planning or executing its programs CHIEFLY because it
    A. allows for the keeping of careful records concerning individual suggestions
    B. lets community leaders know that the agency has regard for their opinions
    C. permits the agency to state in writing which programs seem most appropriate
    D. unifies community leaders against the programs of competing private agencies

25. Good community relations is often action-oriented.
    Which of the following activities of a public agency is LEAST likely to be considered as action-oriented by the people of a local community?
    A. Conducting a survey to gather information about the local community
    B. Extending the use of a facility to those previously excluded
    C. Providing a service that was formerly non-existent
    D. Removing something considered objectionable by the local community

KEY (CORRECT ANSWERS)

1.	A	11.	D
2.	B	12.	B
3.	A	13.	C
4.	B	14.	A
5.	A	15.	B
6.	C	16.	C
7.	A	17.	D
8.	B	18.	D
9.	C	19.	D
10.	D	20.	A

21.	B
22.	A
23.	C
24.	B
25.	A

TEST 2

DIRECTIONS: Each question or incomplete statement is followed by several suggested answers or completions. Select the one that BEST answers the question or completes the statement. *PRINT THE LETTER OF THE CORRECT ANSWER IN THE SPACE AT THE RIGHT.*

1. Methods of communication with employees are of three types: oral, written, and visual.
   A MAJOR advantage of the written word is that it
   A. insures that content will remain unchanged no matter how many persons may be involved in its transmission
   B. facilitates two-way communication in delicate or confidential situations
   C. strengthens chain-of-command procedures in transmission of information and instruction by requiring the use of prescribed channels
   D. encourages the active participation of employees in the solution of complicated problems

   1.____

2. The use of the conference technique in training often requires more preparatory work on the part of the trainer than does a good lecture PRIMARILY because
   A. a conference would cover material of a more technical nature
   B. the trainer will be required to supply more printed material to the participants
   C. a conference usually involves a greater number of trainees
   D. the trainer must be prepared for a wide variety of possible occurrences

   2.____

3. The one of the following which is NOT an advantage of the lecture over most other methods of training is that it can be given
   A. over the radio or on record
   B. to large numbers of trainees
   C. without interruptions
   D. with little preparation

   3.____

4. Of the following, the one which is LEAST appropriate as a purpose for using an employee attitude survey is to
   A. develop a supervisory training program
   B. learn the identity of dissatisfied employees
   C. re-evaluate employee relations policies
   D. re-orient publications designed for employees

   4.____

5. The competent trainer seeks to become knowledgeable both in the work of the agency and in the duties of the positions for which he is to conduct training. Of the following, the GREATEST practical value that result when the trainer gains such knowledge is that
   A. he will be more likely to instruct employees to perform their work in a manner consistent with actual practice
   B. all levels of staff will be favorably impressed by a display of interest in the agency and its work
   C. employees will become familiar with the trainer and will not consider him an outsider
   D. the trainer will gain an accurate picture of the capacity of each employee for training

   5.____

6. Assume that you, the supervisor of a small office, are involved in planning the reorganization of your bureau's work. Management has decided not to inform your staff of the reorganization until the plans are completed.
   If one of your subordinates tells you that he has heard a rumor about reorganization of the department, you should reply that
   A. the reorganization involves the bureau, not the department
   B. you haven't heard anything about departmental reorganization and that he should stop spreading rumors
   C. you will inform your staff at the appropriate time if any definite plans are made involving a reorganization
   D. you do not know what is being planned but will ask your superior for details

7. Of the following training methods, the one in which the trainee's role is usually LEAST active is the _____ method.
   A. case-study
   B. conference
   C. group discussion
   D. lecture

8. Differences in morale between two work groups can sometimes be attributed to differences in the supervision they receive.
   Of the following, the behavior MOST characteristic of a supervisor of a group with high morale is that he
   A. assigns the least difficult tasks to employees with the most seniority
   B. is concerned primarily with his ultimate responsibility, production
   C. delegates authority and responsibility to his staff
   D. is lenient with his workers when they violate rules

9. Informal performance evaluations of individual employees, prepared systematically and regularly over a period of several years, are considered to be useful to a supervisor PRIMARILY because
   A. he will be able to assign tasks based only on these records
   B. unlike formal records, since they are fitted to the characteristics of individual employees, they provide for quick comparisons
   C. he need not discuss them with employees, since they are informal
   D. whatever personnel action he recommends can be substantiated by cumulative records

10. When instructing first-line supervisors in the proper method of evaluating the performance of probationary employees, it is LEAST important for a higher-level supervisor to
    A. explain in detail the standards to be used
    B. inform them of the possibility of higher management review
    C. caution them concerning common errors of evaluation
    D. mention the purposes of probationary employee evaluation

11. Assume that your agency is considering abolishing its official performance rating system but that you, a supervisor of a fairly large office, would like to devise a system for your own use.
The FIRST step in setting up a system would be to
    A. decide what factors and personal characteristics are important and should be rated
    B. compare several rating methods to see which would be easiest to use
    C. have a private conference with each employee to discuss his performance
    D. set specific standards of employee performance, allowing your workers to make suggestions

12. The basic organizational structure of a municipal agency may have come about for several reasons.
Of the following, the MOST important influence on the nature of its structure is the agency's
    A. professional attitude
    B. public reputation
    C. overall goal
    D. staff morale

13. The term *formal organization* refers to that organization structure agreed upon by top management whereas the term *informal organization* refers to the more spontaneous and flexible organizational ties developed by subordinates.
The one of the following which BEST describes the usual *informal organization* is that it represents a(n)
    A. destructive system of relationships which should be eliminated
    B. concealed system of relationships whose goals are the same as management's
    C. actual system of relationships which should be recognized
    D. dysfunctional system of relationships which should be ignored

14. The reluctance of supervisors to delegate work to subordinates when they should is GENERALLY due to the supervisor's
    A. feelings of insecurity in work situations
    B. need to acquire additional experience
    C. inability to exercise control over his subordinates
    D. lack of technical knowledge

15. Assume that you have just been made the supervisor of a group of people you did not know before.
For you to talk casually with each of your new subordinates with the purpose of getting to know them personally would be
    A. *advisable*, chiefly because subordinates have more confidence in a supervisor who shows personal interest in them
    B. *inadvisable*, chiefly because subordinates resent having their supervisor ask about their outside interests
    C. *advisable*, chiefly because one of the supervisor's main concerns should be to help his subordinates with their personal problems
    D. *inadvisable*, chiefly because a supervisor should not allow his relations with his subordinates to be influenced by their personalities

16. It has been found that high-producing subdivisions of organizations usually have supervisors whose behavior is employee-centered, whereas low-producing units usually have supervisors whose behavior is work-centered.
Therefore, it could be concluded from these findings that
    A. a high-producing unit may cause a supervisor to be authoritarian
    B. a low-producing unit may cause a supervisor to be work-centered
    C. close supervision usually increases production
    D. employee-centered leadership may reduce production

17. A recent study in managerial science showed that, as the amount of praise increased and amount of criticism decreased, the supervisor was more likely to be perceived by his subordinates as being
    A. concerned with their career advancement
    B. production oriented, through subtle intimidation
    C. seeking personal satisfaction, irrespective of production
    D. uncertain of the subordinates' reliability

18. The power to issue directives or instructions to employees is derived from employees as much as from management.
It follows MOST logically from this statement that
    A. attitudes toward management can be changed
    B. emphasis on discipline is needed
    C. authority is dependent upon acceptance
    D. employees should be properly supervised for work to be done

19. "In the decision-making process, it is a rare problem that has only one possible solution. Such a solution should be suspected of being nothing but a plausible argument for a preconceived idea."
The author of the foregoing quotation apparently does NOT believe that
    A. there is usually only one possible solution to a problem
    B. the risks involved in any solution should be weighed against expected gains
    C. each alternative should be evaluated to determine the effort needed
    D. actions should be based on the urgency of problems

20. The supervisor who relies on punitive discipline to enforce his authority is putting limits on the potential of his leadership. Fear of punishment may secure obedience, but it destroys initiative. Such a supervisor's autocratic methods have cut off upward communications.
Of the following, the major DISADVANTAGE of such autocratic behavior is that
    A. difficulties in the supervision of his subordinates will arise if limits are placed on the supervisor's responsibility
    B. policies that affect the public will be changed too frequently
    C. the supervisor will apply punishment subjectively rather than objectively
    D. instructions will be obeyed to the letter, regardless of changing circumstances

21. The need for a supervisor to carefully coordinate and direct the work of his unit increases as the work becomes
    A. more routine
    B. more specialized
    C. less complex
    D. less technical

    21.____

22. The MAIN goal of discipline as used by a supervisor should be to
    A. keep the employees' respect
    B. influence behavior, so that work will be completed properly
    C. encourage the employees to work faster
    D. set an example for others

    22.____

23. One of your subordinates has exhibited discourtesy and non-cooperation on several occasions.
    Of the following, the MOST appropriate attitude for you to adopt in dealing with this problem is that
    A. disciplinary measures for such an individual generally creates additional problems
    B. failure to correct such behavior may lead to worse offenses
    C. it is a mistake to make an issue out of minor infractions
    D. the harsher the medicine, the faster the cure

    23.____

24. Assume that an employee has complained to you, his supervisor, that he cannot concentrate on his work because two of his co-workers make too much noise. You pay particular attention to these employees for several days and do not find them making excessive noise.
    The NEXT step you should take in handling this grievance is to
    A. have a talk with all three employees, urging them to cooperate and be considerate of one another
    B. arrange for the complainant to change his work location to a place away from the two co-workers
    C. talk to the complainant to find out if the complaint he made to you is the real cause of his dissatisfaction
    D. tell the complainant that you have found his grievance to be unfounded

    24.____

25. In planning the application of an existing agency program to a local community, it is generally necessary to discover relevant problems and possibilities for service.
    Of the following, the BEST way to learn about such problems and possibilities for service would usually be to
    A. begin the program on a full-scale basis and await reactions
    B. seek opinions and advice from community residents and leaders
    C. hold staff meetings with agency employees who have worked in similar communities
    D. study official federal reports about already completed programs of the same kind

    25.____

KEY (CORRECT ANSWERS)

1.	A	11.	A
2.	D	12.	C
3.	D	13.	C
4.	B	14.	A
5.	A	15.	A
6.	C	16.	B
7.	D	17.	A
8.	C	18.	C
9.	D	19.	A
10.	B	20.	D
21.	B		
22.	B		
23.	B		
24.	C		
25.	B		

TEST 3

DIRECTIONS: Each question or incomplete statement is followed by several suggested answers or completions. Select the one that BEST answers the question or completes the statement. *PRINT THE LETTER OF THE CORRECT ANSWER IN THE SPACE AT THE RIGHT.*

1. Which of the following characteristics would be LEAST detrimental to a supervisor in his efforts to set up and maintain good relations with other supervisors with whom he must deal in the course of his duties?
   A. Not getting involved in consultation on any supervisory problems they might have
   B. Indicating that they should improve their supervising methods and offering suggestions on how to do so
   C. Emphasizing his own role as a member of management
   D. Sharing information which has proved useful in his unit

   1.____

2. Both trainers and supervisors might agree that there is usually a best way to do a particular job. Yet a supervisor or instructor sometimes does not teach a new employee the best way, the most efficient way, to do a complex job.
   Sometimes, in such cases, the supervisor temporarily changes the sequence of operations, increases the number of steps needed to do a job, or makes other changes in the method, which then deviates from the one considered most efficient.
   When is such a difference in approach MOST justified when teaching a new employee a complex job?
   A. When the changes in approach correspond to the learning ability of the new employee
   B. When the new employee's performance on the job is closely supervised to compensate for a change in approach
   C. Where the steps in performing the task have not been defined in a manual of procedures
   D. When the instructor has ideas of improving upon the methods for doing the job

   2.____

3. Considerable thought in the field of management is directed toward the advantages and disadvantages of authoritarian methods of influencing behavior, and, in the so-called authoritarian model, a nucleus of rather consistent ideas prevail.
   Which of the following is LEAST characteristic of an administrative system based on the authoritarian model?
   A. A conviction of a need for order and efficiency in a world consisting mainly of people who lack direction and incentive
   B. Rules and contracts are the basis for action, and decisions are made on an impersonal basis
   C. The right to give orders and instructions is inherent in the hierarchical arrangement of an organizational structure
   D. Realization that subordinates' needs for affiliation and recognition can contribute to management's objectives

   3.____

4. Of the following, the FIRST step in planning an operation is to
   A. obtain relevant information
   B. identify the goal to be achieved
   C. consider possible alternatives
   D. make necessary assignments

5. A supervisor who is extremely busy performing routine tasks is MOST likely making incorrect use of what basis principle of supervision?
   A. Homogeneous Assignment
   B. Span of Control
   C. Work Distribution
   D. Delegation of Authority

6. Controls help supervisors to obtain information from which they can determine whether their staffs are achieving planned goals.
   Which one of the following would be LEAST useful as a control device?
   A. Employee diaries
   B. Organization charts
   C. Periodic inspections
   D. Progress charts

7. A certain employee has difficulty in effectively performing a particular portion of his routine assignments, but his overall productivity is average.
   As a direct supervisor of this individual, your BEST course of action would be to
   A. attempt to develop the investigator's capacity to execute the problematical facets of his assignments
   B. diversify the investigator's work assignments in order to build up his confidence
   C. reassign the investigator to less difficult tasks
   D. request in a private conversation that the investigator improve his work output

8. A supervisor who uses persuasion as a means of supervising a unit would GENERALLY also use which of the following practices to supervise his unit?
   A. Supervises and control the staff with an authoritative attitude to indicate that he is a *take-charge* individual
   B. Make significant changes in the organizational operations so as to improve job efficiency
   C. Remove major communication barriers between himself, subordinates, and management
   D. Supervise everyday operations while being mindful of the problems of his subordinates

9. Whenever a supervisor in charge of a unit delegates a routine task to a capable subordinate, he tells him exactly how to do it.
   This practice is GENERALLY
   A. *desirable*, chiefly because good supervisors should be aware of the traits of their subordinates and delegate responsibilities to them accordingly
   B. *undesirable*, chiefly because only non-routine tasks should be delegated
   C. *desirable*, chiefly because a supervisor should frequently test the willingness of his subordinates to perform ordinary tasks
   D. *undesirable*, chiefly because a capable subordinate should usually be allowed to exercise his own discretion in doing a routine job

10. The one of the following activities through which a supervisor BEST demonstrates leadership ability is by
    A. arranging periodic staff meetings in order to keep his subordinates informed about professional developments in the field of investigation
    B. frequently issuing definite orders and directives which will lessen the need for subordinates to make decisions in handling any investigations assigned to them
    C. devoting the major part of his time to supervising subordinates so as to stimulate continuous improvement
    D. setting aside time for self-development and research so as to improve the investigative techniques and procedures of his unit

11. The following three statements relate to supervision of employees:
    I. The assignment of difficult tasks that offer a challenge is more conducive to good morale than the assignment of easy tasks.
    II. The same general principles of supervision that apply to men are equally applicable to women.
    III. The best restraining program should cover all phases of an employee's work in a general manner.
    Which of the following choices lists ALL of the above statements that are generally CORRECT?
    A. II, III   B. I   C. I, II   D. I, II, III

12. Which of the following examples BEST illustrates the application of the *exception principle* as a supervisory technique? A(n)
    A. complex job is divided among several employees who work simultaneously to complete the whole job in a shorter time
    B. employee is required to complete any task delegated to him to such an extent that nothing is left for the superior who delegated the task except to approve it
    C. superior delegates responsibility to a subordinate but retains authority to make the final decisions
    D. superior delegates all work possible to his subordinates and retains that which requires his personal attention or performance

13. Assume that you are a supervisor. Your immediate superior frequently gives orders to your subordinates without your knowledge.
    Of the following, the MOST direct and effective way for you to handle this problem is to
    A. tell your subordinates to take orders only from you
    B. submit a report to higher authority in which you cite specific instances
    C. discuss it with your immediate superior
    D. find out to what extent you authority and prestige as a supervisor have been affected

14. In an agency which has as its primary purpose the protection of the public against fraudulent business practices, which of the following would GENERALLY be considered an auxiliary or staff rather than a line function?

A. Interviewing victims of frauds and advising them about their legal remedies
B. Daily activities directed toward prevention of fraudulent business practices
C. Keeping records and statistics about business violations reported and corrected
D. Follow-up inspections by investigators after corrective action has been taken

15. A supervisor can MOST effectively reduce the spread of false rumors through the *grapevine* by
    A. identifying and disciplining any subordinate responsible for initiating such rumors
    B. keeping his subordinates informed as much as possible about matters affecting them
    C. denying false rumors which might tend to lower staff morale and productivity
    D. making sure confidential matters are kept secure from access by unauthorized employees

16. A supervisor has tried to learn about the background, education, and family relationships of his subordinates through observation, personal contact, and inspection of their personnel records.
    These supervisory actions are GENERALLY
    A. *inadvisable*, chiefly because they may lead to charges of favoritism
    B. *advisable*, chiefly because they may make him more popular with his subordinates
    C. *inadvisable*, chiefly because his efforts may be regarded as an invasion of privacy
    D. *advisable*, chiefly because the information may enable him to develop better understanding of each of his subordinates

17. In an emergency situation, when action must be taken immediately, it is BEST for the supervisor to give orders in the form of
    A. direct commands, which are brief and precise
    B. requests, so that his subordinate will not become alarmed
    C. suggestions, which offer alternative courses of action
    D. implied directive, so that his subordinates may use their judgment in carrying them out

18. When demonstrating a new and complex procedure to a group of subordinates, it is ESSENTIAL that a supervisor
    A. go slowly and repeat the steps involved at least once
    B. show the employees common errors and the consequences of such errors
    C. go through the process at the usual speed so that the employees can see the rate at which they should work
    D. distribute summaries of the procedure during the demonstration and instruct his subordinates to refer to them afterwards

19. The PRIMARY value of office reports and procedures is to
    A. assist top management in controlling key agency functions
    B. measure job performance
    C. save time and labor
    D. control the activities and use of time of all staff members

    19.____

20. Of the following, which is considered to be the GREATEST advantage of the oral report? It
    A. allows for accurate transmission of information from one individual to another
    B. presents an opportunity to discuss or clarify any immediate questions raised by the receiver of the report
    C. requires less office work to maintain records on actions taken when an oral report is involved
    D. takes only a short amount of time to plan and prepare material for an oral report

    20.____

21. A supervisor who is to make a report about a job he has done can make an oral report of a written report.
    Of the following, which is the BEST time to make an oral report? When
    A. the work covers an emergency situation
    B. a record is needed for the files
    C. the report is channeled to other departments
    D. the report covers additional work he will do

    21.____

22. Suppose that a new employee has been assigned to you. It is your responsibility to see to it that he understands how to fill out properly the forms he is required to use.
    What would be the BEST way to do this?
    A. Explain the use of each form to the new technician and show him how to fill them out
    B. Give the new employee a copy of each form he must use so that he can learn by studying them
    C. Ask an experienced worker to explain clearly to him how the forms should be filled out
    D. Tell the new employee that filling out forms is simple and he should follow the instructions on each form

    22.____

23. As a supervisor, you want to have your staff take part in improving work methods.
    Of the following, the BEST way to do this is to
    A. make critical appraisals of their work frequently
    B. encourage them to make suggestions
    C. make no change without their approval
    D. hold regular staff meetings

    23.____

24. A good relationship with other supervisors is important to a senior supervisor. Close cooperation among supervisory personnel is MOST likely to result in
    A. increasing the probability for support of supervisory actions and decisions
    B. stimulating supervisors to achieve higher status in the organization
    C. helping to control the flow of work within a unit
    D. a clearer definition of the responsibilities of individual supervisors

25. Which of the following is MOST likely to gain a supervisor the respect and cooperation of his staff?
    A. Assigning the most difficult jobs to the experienced staff members
    B. Giving each staff member the same number of assignments
    C. Assigning jobs according to each staff member's ability
    D. Giving each staff member the same types of assignments

KEY (CORRECT ANSWERS)

1.	D	11.	C
2.	A	12.	D
3.	D	13.	C
4.	B	14.	C
5.	D	15.	B
6.	B	16.	D
7.	A	17.	A
8.	D	18.	A
9.	D	19.	A
10.	C	20.	B

21. A
22. A
23. B
24. A
25. C

EXAMINATION SECTION
TEST 1

DIRECTIONS: Each question or incomplete statement is followed by several suggested answers or completions. Select the one that BEST answers the question or completes the statement. *PRINT THE LETTER OF THE CORRECT ANSWER IN THE SPACE AT THE RIGHT.*

1. A supervisor was given a booklet that showed a new work method that could save time. He didn't tell his men because he thought that they would get the booklet anyway.
   For the supervisor to have acted like this is a
   A. *good* idea, because he saves time and both of talking to the men
   B. *bad* idea, because he should make sure his men know about better work methods
   C. *good* idea, because the men would rather read about it themselves
   D. *bad* idea, because a supervisor should always show his men every memo he gets from higher authority

    1.____

2. A supervisor found it necessary to discipline two subordinates. One man had been operating his equipment in a wrong way, while the other man came to work late for three days in a row. The supervisor decided to talk to both men together.
   For the supervisor to deal with the problems in this way is a
   A. *good* idea because each man will learn about the difficulties of the other person and how to solve such difficulties
   B. *bad* idea because the supervisor should wait until he can bring a larger group together and save time in discussing such questions
   C. *good* idea because he will be able to get the men to see that their problems are related
   D. *bad* idea because he should meet with each man separately and give him his full attention

    2.____

3. A supervisor should try to make his men feel their jobs are important in order to
   A. get the men to say good things about their supervisor to his own superior
   B. get the men to think in terms of advancing to better jobs
   C. let higher management in the agency know that the supervisor is efficient
   D. help the men to be able to work more efficiently and enthusiastically

    3.____

4. A supervisor should know approximately how long it takes to do a particular kind of job CHIEFLY because he
   A. will know how much time to take if he has to do it himself
   B. will be able to tell his men to do it even faster
   C. can judge the performance of the person doing the job
   D. can retrain experienced employees in better work habits

    4.____

5. Supervisors often get their employees' opinions about better work methods because
   A. the men will know that they are respected
   B. the men would otherwise lose all their confidence in the supervisor
   C. the supervisor might find in this way a good suggestion he could use
   D. this is the best method for improvement of work methods

6. Right after you have trained your subordinates in doing a new job, you find that they seem to be doing all right, but that it will take them several days to finish. You also have several groups of men working at other locations.
   The MOST efficient way for you to make sure that the men continue doing the new job properly is to
   A. stay on that job with the men until it is finished just in case trouble develops
   B. visit the men every half hour until the job is done
   C. stay away from their job that day and visit the men the next day to ask them if they had any problems
   D. visit the men a few times each day until they finish the new job

7. Assume that one of your new employees is older than you are. You also think that he may be hard to get along with because he is older than you.
   The BEST way for you to avoid any problems with the older worker is for you to
   A. lay down the law immediately and tell the man he better not cause you any trouble
   B. treat the man just the way you would any other worker
   C. always ask the older worker for advice in the presence of all the men
   D. ignore the man entirely until he realizes that you are the boss

8. Assume that you have tried a new method suggested by one of your employees and find that it is easier and cheaper than the method you had been using.
   The PROPER thing for you to do NEXT is to
   A. say nothing to anyone but train your men to use the new method
   B. train your men to use the new method and tell your crew that you got the idea from one of the men
   C. continue using the old method because a supervisor should not use suggestions of his men
   D. have your crew learn the new method and take credit for the idea since you are the boss

9. Suppose you are a supervisor and your superior tells you that the way your men are doing a certain procedure is wrong and that you should re-train our men as soon as possible.
   When you begin to re-train the men, the FIRST thing you should do is to
   A. tell your men that a wrong procedure had been used and that a new method must be learned as a result
   B. train your employees in the new method with no explanation since you are the boss

C. tell the crew that your superior has just decided that everyone should learn a new method
D. tell the crew that your superior says your method is wrong but that you don't agree with this

10. It is BAD practice to criticize a man in front of the other men because
    A. people will think you are too strict
    B. it is annoying to anyone who walks by
    C. it is embarrassing to the man concerned
    D. it will antagonize the other men

10.____

11. A supervisor decides not to put his two best men on a work detail because he knows that they won't like it.
    For the supervisor to make the work assignment this way is a
    A. *good* idea because it is only fair to give your best men a break once in a while
    B. *bad* idea because you should treat all of your me fairly and not show favoritism
    C. *good* idea because you save the strength of these men for another job
    D. *bad* idea because more of the men should be exempted from the assignment

11.____

12. Suppose you are a supervisor and you find it inconvenient to obey an established procedure set by your agency. You think another procedure would be better.
    The BEST thing to do first about this procedure that you don't like is for you to
    A. obey the procedure even if you don't to and suggest your idea to your own supervisor
    B. disregard the procedure because a supervisor is supposed to have some privileges
    C. follow the procedure some of the time but ignore it when the men are not watching
    D. organize a group of other supervisors to get the procedure changed

12.____

13. A supervisor estimated that it would take his crew one workday per week to do a certain job each week. However, after a month he noticed that the job averaged two and a half days a week and this delayed other jobs that had to be done.
    The FIRST thing that the supervisor should do in this case is to
    A. call him men together and warn them that they will get a poor work evaluation if they do not work harder
    B. talk to each man personally, asking him to work harder on the job
    C. go back and study the maintenance job by himself to see if more men should be assigned to the job
    D. write his boss a report describing in detail how much time it is taking the men to do the job

13.____

14. An employee complains to you that some of the work assignments are too difficult to do alone.
Which of the following is the BEST way for you to handle this complaint?
    A. Go with him to see exactly what he does and why he finds it so difficult
    B. Politely tell the man that he has to do the job or be brought up on charges
    C. Tell the man to send his complaint to the head of your agency
    D. Sympathize with the man and give him easier jobs

15. The BEST way for a supervisor to keep control of his work assignments is to
    A. ask the men to report to him immediately when their jobs are finished
    B. walk around the buildings once a week and get a first-hand view of what is being done
    C. keep his ears open for problems and complaints, but leave the men aloe to do the work
    D. write up a work schedule and check it periodically against the actual work done

16. A supervisor made a work schedule for his men. At the bottom of it, he wrote, *No changes or exceptions will be made in this schedule for any reason.*
For the supervisor to have made this statement is
    A. *good*, because the men will respect the supervisor for his attitude
    B. *bad*, because there are emergencies and special situations that occur
    C. *good*, because each man will know exactly what is expected of him
    D. *bad*, because the men should expect that no changes will ever be made in the work schedule without written permission

17. Which one of the following would NOT be a result of a well-planned work schedule?
The schedule
    A. makes efficient use of the time of the staff
    B. acts as a checklist for an important job that might be left out
    C. will give an idea of the work to a substitute supervisor
    D. shows at a glance who the best men are

18. A new piece of equipment you have ordered is delivered. You are familiar with it, but the men under you who will use it do not know the equipment.
Of the following methods, which is the BEST to take in explaining to them how to operate this equipment?
    A. Ask the men to watch other crews using the equipment
    B. Show one reliable man how to operate the equipment and ask him to teach the other men
    C. Ask the men to read the instructions in the manual for the equipment
    D. Call the men together and show them how to operate the equipment

19. One supervisor assigns work to his men by calling his crew together each week and describing what has to be done that week. He then tells them to arrange individual assignments among themselves and to work as a team during the week.

This method of scheduling work is a
- A. *good* idea because this guarantees that the men will work together
- B. *bad* idea because responsibility for doing the job is poorly fixed
- C. *good* idea because the men will finish the job in less time, working together
- D. *bad* idea because the supervisor should always stay with his men

20. Suppose that an employee came to his supervisor with a problem concerning his assignment.
    For the supervisor to listen to his problem is a
    - A. *good* idea because a supervisor should always take time off to talk when one of his men wants to talk
    - B. *bad* idea because the supervisor should not be bothered during the work day
    - C. *good* idea because it is the job of the supervisor to deal with problems of job assignment
    - D. *bad* idea because the employee could start annoying the supervisor with all sorts of problems

21. Suppose that on the previous afternoon you were looking for an experienced employee in order to give him an emergency job and he was missing from his job location. The next morning, he tells you that he got sick suddenly and had to go home, but could not tell you since you were not around. He has never done this before.
    What should you do?
    - A. Tell the man he is excused and that in such circumstances he did the wisest thing
    - B. Bring the man up on charges because whatever he says he could still have notified you
    - C. Have the man examined by a doctor to see if he really was sick the day before
    - D. Explain to the mean that he should make every effort to tell you or to get a message to you if he must leave

22. An employee had a grievance and went to his supervisor about it. The employee was not satisfied with the way the supervisor tried to help him and told him so. Yet, the supervisor had done everything he could under the circumstances.
    The PROPER action for the supervisor to take at this time is to
    - A. politely tell the employee that there is nothing more for the supervisor to do about the problem
    - B. let the employee know how he can bring his complaint to a higher authority
    - C. tell the employee that he must solve the problem on his own since he did not want to follow the supervisor's advice
    - D. suggest to the employee that he ask for another supervisor for assistance

23. In which of the following situations is it BEST to give your men spoken rather than written orders?
    A. You want your men to have a record of the instructions.
    B. Spoken instructions are less likely to be forgotten.
    C. An emergency situation has arisen in which there is no time to write up instructions.
    D. There are instructions on time and leave regulations which are complicated.

24. One of your employees tells you that a week ago he had a small accident on the job but he did not bother telling you because he was able to continue working.
    For the employee not to have told his supervisor about the accident was
    A. *good*, because the accident was a small one
    B. *bad*, because all accidents should be reported, no matter how small
    C. *good*, because the supervisor should be bothered only for important matters
    D. *bad*, because having an accident is one way to get excused for the day

25. For a supervisor to deal with each of his subordinate in exactly the same manner is
    A. *poor*, because each man presents a different problem and there is no one way of handling all problems
    B. *good*, because once a problem is handled with one man, he can handle another man with the same problem
    C. *poor*, because the men will resent it if they are not handled each in a better way than others
    D. *good*, because this assures fair and impartial treatment of each subordinate

KEY (CORRECT ANSWERS)

1.	B	11.	B
2.	D	12.	A
3.	D	13.	C
4.	C	14.	A
5.	C	15.	D
6.	D	16.	B
7.	B	17.	D
8.	B	18.	D
9.	A	19.	B
10.	C	20.	C

21.	D
22.	B
23.	C
24.	B
25.	A

TEST 2

DIRECTIONS: Each question or incomplete statement is followed by several suggested answers or completions. Select the one that BEST answers the question or completes the statement. *PRINT THE LETTER OF THE CORRECT ANSWER IN THE SPACE AT THE RIGHT.*

1. Jim Johnson has been on your staff for over four years. He has always been a conscientious and productive worker. About a month ago, his wife died; and since that time, his work performance has been very poor.
   As his supervisor, which one of the following is the BEST way for you to deal with this situation?
   A. Allow Jim as much time as he needs to overcome his grief and hope that his work performance improves
   B. Meet with Jim to discuss ways to improve his performance
   C. Tell Jim directly that you are more concerned with his work performance than with his personal problem
   D. Prepare disciplinary action on Jim as soon as possible

   1.____

2. You are responsible for the overall operation of a storehouse which is divided into two sections. Each section has its own supervisor. You have decided to make several complex changes in the storekeeping procedures which will affect both sections.
   Of the following, the BEST way to make sure that these changes are understood by the two supervisors is for you to
   A. meet with both supervisors to discuss the changes
   B. issue a memorandum to each supervisor explaining the changes
   C. post the changes where the supervisors are sure to see them
   D. instruct one supervisor to explain the changes to the other supervisor

   2.____

3. You have called a meeting of all your subordinates to tell them what has to be done on a new project in which they will all be involved. Several times during the meeting, you ask if there are any questions about what you have told them.
   Of the following, to ask the subordinates whether there are any questions during the meeting can BEST be described as
   A. *inadvisable*, because it interferes with their learning about the new project
   B. *advisable*, because you will find out what they don't understand and have a chance to clear up any problems they may have
   C. *inadvisable*, because it makes the meeting too long and causes the subordinates to lose interest in the new project
   D. *advisable*, because it gives you a chance to learn which of your subordinates are paying attention to what you say

   3.____

4. As a supervisor, you are responsible for seeing to it that absenteeism does not become a problem among your subordinates.
   Which one of the following is NOT an acceptable way of controlling the problem of excessive absences?

   4.____

A. Distribute a written statement to your staff on the policies regarding absenteeism in your organization
B. Arrange for workers who have the fewest absences to talk to those workers who have the most absences
C. Let your subordinates know that a record is being kept of all absences
D. Arrange for counseling of those employees who are frequently absent

5. One of your supervisors has been an excellent worker for the past two years. There are no promotion opportunities for this worker in the foreseeable future. Due to the city's present budget crisis, a salary increase is not possible. Under the circumstances, which one of the following actions on your part would be MOST likely to continue to motivate this worker?
    A. Tell the worker that times are bad all over and jobs are hard to find
    B. Give the worker less work and easier assignments
    C. Tell the worker to try to look for a better paying job elsewhere
    D. Seek the worker's advice often and show that the suggestions provided are appreciated

6. As a supervisor in a warehouse, it is important that you use your available work force to its fullest potential.
Which one of the following actions on your part is MOST likely to increase the effectiveness of your work force?
    A. Assigning more workers to a job than the number actually needed
    B. Eliminating all job training to allow more time for work output
    C. Using your best workers on jobs that average workers can do
    D. Making sure that all materials and equipment used are maintained in good working order

7. You learn that your storage area will soon be undergoing changes which will affect the work of your subordinates. You decide not to tell your subordinates about what is to happen.
Of the following, your action can BEST be described as
    A. *wise*, because your subordinates will learn of the changes for themselves
    B. *unwise*, because your subordinates should be advised about what is to happen
    C. *wise*, because it is better for your subordinates to continue working without being disturbed by such news
    D. *unwise*, because the work of your subordinates will gradually slow down

8. In making plans for the operation of your unit, you are MOST likely to see these plans carried out successfully if you
    A. allow your staff to participate in developing these plans
    B. do not spend any time on the minor details of these plans
    C. base these plans on the past experiences of others
    D. allow these plans to interact with outside activities in other units

9. As a supervisor in charge of the total operation of a food supply warehouse, you find vandalism to be a potentially serious problem. On occasion, trespassers have gained entrance into the facility by climbing over an unprotected 8-foot fence surrounding the warehouse whose dimensions measure 100 feet by 100 feet.
Assuming that all of the following would be equally effective ways in preventing these breaches in security in the situation described above, which one would be LEAST costly?
   A. Using two trained guard dogs to roam freely throughout the facility at night
   B. Hiring a security guard to patrol the facility after working hours
   C. Installing tape razor wire on top of the fence surrounding the facility
   D. Installing an electronic burglar alarm system requiring the installation of a new fence

10. The area for which you have program responsibility has undergone recent changes. Your staff is now required to perform many new tasks, and morale is low.
The LEAST effective way for you to improve long-term staff morale would be to
   A. develop support groups to discuss problems
   B. involve staff in job development
   C. maintain a comfortable social environment within the group
   D. adequately plan and give assignments in a timely manner

11. As a supervisor in a large office, one of your subordinate supervisors stops you in the middle of the office and complains loudly that he is being treated unfairly. The rest of the staff ceases work and listens to the complaint.
The MOST appropriate action for you to take in this situation is to
   A. ignore this unprofessional behavior and continue on your way
   B. tell the supervisor that his behavior is unprofessional and he should learn how to conduct himself
   C. explain to the supervisor why you believe he is not being treated unfairly
   D. ask the supervisor to come to your office at a specific time to discuss the matter

12. You are told that one of your subordinates is distributing literature which attempts to recruit individuals to join a particular organization. Several workers complain that their rights are being violated.
Of the following, the BEST action for you to take FIRST is to
   A. ignore the situation because no harm is being done
   B. discuss the matter further with your supervisor
   C. ask the worker to stop distributing the literature
   D. tell the workers that they do not have to read the material

13. You have been assigned to develop a short training course for a recently issued procedure.
In designing this course, which of the following statements is the LEAST important for you to consider?

A. The learning experience must be interesting and meaningful in terms of the staff member's job.
B. The method of teaching must be strictly followed in order to develop successful learning experiences.
C. The course content should incorporate the rules and regulations of the agency.
D. The procedure should be consistent with the agency's objectives.

14. As a supervisor, there are several newly-promoted employees under your supervision. Each of these employees is subject to a probationary period PRIMARILY to
    A. assess the employee's performance to see if the employee should be retained or removed from the position
    B. give the employee the option to return to his former employment if the employee is unhappy in the new position
    C. give the employee an opportunity to learn the duties and responsibilities of the position
    D. judge the employee's potential for upward mobility in the future

15. An employee under your supervision rushes into your office to tell you he has just received a telephone bomb threat.
    As the administrative supervisor, the FIRST thing you should do is
    A. evacuate staff from the floor
    B. call the police and building security
    C. advise your administrator
    D. do a preliminary search

16. After reviewing the Absence Control form for a unit under your supervision, you find that one of your staff members has a fifth undocumented sick leave within a six-month period.
    In this situation, the FIRST action you should take is to
    A. discuss the seriousness of the matter with the staff member when he returns to work and fully document the details of the discussion
    B. review the case with the location director and warn the staff member that future use of sick leave will be punished
    C. submit the proper disciplinary forms to ensure that the staff member is penalized for excessive absences
    D. request that the timekeeper put the staff member on doctor's note restriction

17. A subordinate supervisor recently assigned to your office begins his first conference with you by saying that he has learned something that another supervisor is doing that you should know about.
    After hearing this statement, of the following, the BEST approach for you to take is to
    A. explain to the supervisor that the conference is to discuss his work and not that of his co-workers
    B. tell the supervisor that you do not encourage a spy system among the staff you supervise

C. tell the supervisor that you will listen to his report only if the other supervisor is present
D. allow the supervisor to continue talking until you have enough information to make a decision on how best to respond

18. Assume that you are a supervisor recently assigned to a new unit. You notice that, for the past few days, one of the employees in your unit whose work is about average has been stopping work at about four o'clock and has been spending the rest of the afternoon relaxing at his desk.
The BEST of the following actions for you to take in this situation is to
A. assign more work to this employee since it is apparent that he does not have enough work to keep him busy
B. observe the employee's conduct more closely for about ten days before taking any more positive action
C. discuss the matter with the employee, pointing out to him how he can use the extra hour daily to raise the level of his job performance
D. question the previous supervisor in charge of the unit in order to determine whether he had sanctioned such conduct when he supervised that unit

19. A new supervisor was assigned to your program four months ago. Although he tries hard, he has been unable to meet certain standards because he still has a lot to learn. As his supervisor, you are required to submit performance evaluations within a few days.
How would you rate this employee on the tasks where he fails to meet standards because of lack of experience?
A. Satisfactory
B. Conditional
C. Unsatisfactory
D. Unratable

20. You find that there is an important procedural error in a memo which you distributed to your staff several days ago.
The BEST approach for you to take at this time is to
A. send a corrected memo to the staff, indicating what prior error was made
B. send a corrected memo to the staff without mentioning the prior error
C. tell the staff about the error at the next monthly staff meeting
D. place the corrected memo on the office bulletin board

21. Your superior asks you, a supervisor, about the status of the response to a letter from a public official concerning a client's case. When you ask the subordinate who was assigned to prepare the response to give you the letter, the subordinate denies that it was given to him. You are certain that the subordinate has the letter, but is withholding it because the response has not yet been prepared.
Of the following, in order to secure the letter from the subordinate, you should FIRST
A. accuse the subordinate of lying and demand that the letter be given to you immediately
B. say that you would consider it a personal favor if the subordinate would find the letter

6 (#2)

  C. continue to question the subordinate until he admits to having been given the letter
  D. offer a face-saving solution, such as asking the subordinate to look again for the letter

22. As a supervisor, you have been assigned to write a few paragraphs to be included in the agency's annual report, describing a public service agency department this year as compared to last year.
Which of the following elements basic to the agency is LEAST likely to have changed since last year?
  A. Mission B. Structure C. Technology D. Personnel

23. As a supervisor, you have been informed that a grievance has been filed against you, accusing you of assigning a subordinate to out-of-title tasks.
Of the following, the BEST approach for you to take is to
  A. waive the grievance so that it will proceed to a Step II hearing
  B. immediately change the subordinate's assignment to avoid future problems
  C. respond to the grievance, giving appropriate reasons for the assignment
  D. review the job description to ensure that the subordinate's tasks are not out-of-title

24. Which of the following is NOT a correct statement about agency group training programs in a public service agency?
  A. Training sessions continue for an indefinite period of time.
  B. Group training sessions are planned for designated personnel.
  C. Training groups are organized formally through administrative planning.
  D. Group training is task-centered and aimed toward accomplishing specific educational goals.

25. As a supervisor, you have submitted a memo to your superior requesting a conference to discuss the performance of a manager under your supervision. The memo states that the manager has a good working relationship with her staff; however, she tends to interpret agency policy too liberally and shows poor administrative skills by missing some deadlines and not keeping proper controls.
Which of the following steps should NOT be taken in order to prepare for this conference with your superior?
  A. Collect and review all your notes regarding the manager's prior performance.
  B. Outline your agenda so that you will have sufficient time to discuss the situation.
  C. Tell the manager that you will be discussing her performance with your superior.
  D. Clearly define objectives which will focus on improving the manager's performance.

KEY (CORRECT ANSWERS)

1.	B		11.	D
2.	A		12.	C
3.	B		13.	B
4.	B		14.	A
5.	D		15.	B
6.	D		16.	A
7.	B		17.	D
8.	A		18.	C
9.	C		19.	B
10.	C		20.	A

21. D
22. A
23. C
24. A
25. C

READING COMPREHENSION
UNDERSTANDING WRITTEN MATERIALS

COMMENTARY

The ability to read and understand written materials—texts, publications, newspapers, orders, directions, expositions—is a skill basic to a functioning democracy and to an efficient business or viable government.

That is why almost all examinations—for beginning, middle, and senior levels—test reading comprehension, directly or indirectly.

The reading test measures how well you understand what you read. This is how it is done: You read a passage followed by several statements. From these statements, you choose the one statement, or answer, that is BEST supported by, or BEST matches, what is said in the paragraph. PRINT THE LETTER OF THE CORRECT ANSWER IN THE SPACE AT THE RIGHT.

SAMPLE QUESTIONS

DIRECTIONS: Answer Questions 1 and 2 ONLY according to the information given in the following passage.

1. When a fingerprint technician inks and takes rolled impressions of a subject's fingers, the degree of downward pressure the technician applies is important. The correct pressure may best be determined through experience and observation. It is quite important, however, that the subject be cautioned to relax and not help the fingerprint technician by also applying pressure, as this prevents the fingerprint technician from gaging the amount needed. A method which is helpful in getting the subject to relax his hand is to instruct him to look at some distant object and not to look at his hands.

1. According to this passage, the technician tries to relax the subject's hands by
    A. instructing him to let his hands hang loosely
    B. telling him that being fingerprinted is painless
    C. asking him to look at this hand instead of some distant object
    D. asking him to look at something other than his hand

2. The subject is asked NOT to press down on his fingers while being fingerprinted because
    A. the impressions taken become rolled
    B. the subject may apply too little downward pressure and spoil the impressions
    C. the technician cannot tell whether he is applying the right degree of pressure
    D. he doesn't have the experience to apply the exact amount of pressure

CORRECT ANSWERS
1. D
2. C

EXAMINATION SECTION
TEST 1

DIRECTIONS: Questions 1 through 3 are to be answered on the basis of the following reading passage. *PRINT THE LETTER OF THE CORRECT ANSWER IN THE SPACE AT THE RIGHT.*

Thermostats should be tested in hot water for proper opening. A bucket should be filled with sufficient water to cover the thermostat and fitted with a thermometer suspended in the water so that the sensitive bulb portion does not rest directly on the bucket. The water is then heated on a stove. As the temperature of the water passes the 160-165° range, the thermostat should start to open and should be completely opened when the temperature has risen to 185-190°. Lifting the thermostat into the air should cause a pronounced closing action and the unit should be closed entirely within a short time.

1. The thermostat described above is a device which opens and closes with changes in the
   A. position   B. pressure   C. temperature   D. surroundings

   1._____

2. According to the above passage, the closing action of the thermostat should be tested by
   A. working the thermostat back and forth
   B. permitting the water to cool gradually
   C. adding cold water to the bucket
   D. removing the thermostat from the bucket

   2._____

3. The bulb of the thermometer should not rest directly on the bucket because
   A. the bucket gets hotter than the water
   B. the thermometer might be damaged in that position
   C. it is difficult to read the thermometer in that position
   D. the thermometer might interfere with operation of the thermostat

   3._____

KEY (CORRECT ANSWERS)

1. C
2. D
3. A

TEST 2

DIRECTIONS: Questions 1 through 3 are to be answered on the basis of the following reading passage. *PRINT THE LETTER OF THE CORRECT ANSWER IN THE SPACE AT THE RIGHT.*

All idle pumps should be turned daily by hand, and should be run under power at least once a week. Whenever repairs are made on a pump, a record should be kept so that it will be possible to judge the success with which the pump is performing its functions. If a pump fails to deliver liquid, there may be an obstruction in the suction line, the pump's parts may be badly worn, or the packing defective.

1. According to the above passage, pumps 1.____
   A. in use should be turned by hand every day
   B. which are not in use should be run under power every day
   C. which are in daily use should be run under power several times a week
   D. which are not in use should be turned by hand every day

2. According to the above passage, the reason for keeping records of repairs made on pumps is to 2.____
   A. make certain that proper maintenance is being performed
   B. discover who is responsible for improper repairs
   C. rate the performance of the pumps
   D. know when to replace worn parts

3. The one of the following causes of pump failure which is NOT mentioned in the above passage is 3.____
   A. excessive suction lift B. clogged lines
   C. bad packing D. worn parts

KEY (CORRECT ANSWERS)

1. A
2. C
3. A

TEST 3

DIRECTIONS: Questions 1 through 5 are to be answered on the basis of the following reading passage. *PRINT THE LETTER OF THE CORRECT ANSWER IN THE SPACE AT THE RIGHT.*

Floors in warehouses, storerooms, and shipping rooms must be strong enough to stay level under heavy loads. Unevenness of floors may cause boxes of materials to topple and fall. Safe floor load capacities and maximum heights to which boxes may be stacked should be posted conspicuously so all can notice it. Where material in boxes, containers, or cartons of the same weight is regularly stored, it is good practice to paint a horizontal line on the wall indicating the maximum height to which the material may be piled. A qualified expert should determine floor load capacity from the building plans, the age and condition of the floor supports, the type of floor, and other related information.

Working aisles are those from which material is placed into and removed from storage. Working aisles are of two types: transportation aisles, running the length of the building, and cross aisles, running across the width of the building. Deciding on the number, width, and location of working aisles is important. While aisles are necessary and determine boundaries of storage areas, they reduce the space actually used for storage.

1. According to the above passage, how should safe floor load capacities be made known to employees? They should be
    A. given out to each employee
    B. given to supervisors only
    C. printed in large red letters
    D. posted so that they are easily seen

2. According to the above passage, floor load capacities should be determined by
    A. warehouse supervisors
    B. the fire department
    C. qualified experts
    D. machine operators

3. According to the above passage, transportation aisles
    A. run the length of the building
    B. run across the width of the building
    C. are wider than cross aisles
    D. are shorter than cross aisles

4. According to the above passage, working aisles tend to
    A. take away space that could be used for storage
    B. add to space that could be used for storage
    C. slow down incoming stock
    D. speed up outgoing stock

5. According to the above passage, unevenness of floors may cause
    A. overall warehouse deterioration
    B. piles of stock to fall
    C. materials to spoil
    D. many worker injuries

KEY (CORRECT ANSWERS)

1. D
2. C
3. A
4. A
5. B

TEST 4

DIRECTIONS: Questions 1 through 3 are to be answered on the basis of the following reading passage. *PRINT THE LETTER OF THE CORRECT ANSWER IN THE SPACE AT THE RIGHT.*

In a retail establishment, any overweight means a distinct loss to the merchant, and even an apparently inconsequential overweight on a single package or sale when multiplied by the total number of transactions, could run into large figures. In addition to the use of reliable scales and weights, and their maintenance in proper condition, there must be proper supervision of the selling force. Such supervision is a difficult matter, particularly on the score of carelessness, as the depositing of extra amounts of material on the scale and failure to remove the same when it overbalances the scale may become a habit. In case of underweight, either in the weighing or by the use of fraudulent scales and weights, the seller soon will hear of it, but there is no reason why the amount weighed out should be in excess of what the customer pays for. Checking sales records against invoices and inventories can supply some indication of the tendency of the sales force to become careless in this field.

1. Of the following, the MOST valid implication of the above passage is that
    A. all overweights which occur in retail stores are in small amounts
    B. even-arm and uneven-arm balances and weights which are unreliable lead more often to underweights than to overweights
    C. overweights due to errors of salesclerks necessarily lead to large losses by a retailer
    D. supervision to prevent overweights is more important to a retailer than remedial measures after their occurrence

1.____

2. Of the following, the MOST valid implication of the above passage is that
    A. depositing of insufficient amounts of commodities on scales and failure to add to them may become a habit with salesclerks
    B. salesclerks should be trained in understanding and maintenance of scale mechanisms
    C. supervision of salesclerks to prevent careless habits in weighing must depend upon personal observation

2.____

3. According to the above passage, the MOST accurate of the following statements is:
    A. For the most part, the ideas expressed in the passage do not apply to wholesale establishments.
    B. Inventories of commodities prepacked in the store are the only ones which can be used in checking losses due to overweight.
    C. Invoices which give the value and weight of merchandise received are useful in checking losses due to overweights.
    D. The principal value of inventories is to indicate losses due to overweights.

3.____

KEY (CORRECT ANSWERS)

1. D
2. C
3. C

TEST 5

DIRECTIONS: Questions 1 through 5 are to be answered on the basis of the following reading passage. *PRINT THE LETTER OF THE CORRECT ANSWER IN THE SPACE AT THE RIGHT.*

TITANIC AIR COMPRESSOR

Valves: The compressors are equipped with Titanic plate valves which are automatic in operation. Valves are so constructed that an entire valve assembly can readily be removed from the head. The valves provide large port areas with short lift and are accurately guided to insure positive seating.

Starting Unloader: Each compressor (or air end) is equipped with a centrifugal governor which is bolted directly to the compressor crank shaft. The governor actuates cylinder relief valves so as to relieve pressure from the cylinders during starting and stopping. The motor is never required to start the compressor tinder load.

Air Strainer: Each cylinder air inlet connection is fitted with a suitable combination air strainer and muffler.

Pistons: Pistons are lightweight castings, ribbed internally to secure strength, and are accurately turned and ground. Each piston is fitted with four (4) rings, two of which are oil control rings. Piston pins are hardened and tempered steel of the full floating type. Bronze bushings are used between piston pin and piston

Connecting Rods: Connecting rods are of solid bronze designed for maximum strength, rigidity, and wear. Crank pins are fitted with renewable steel bushings. Connecting rods are of the one-piece type, there being no bolts, nuts, or cotter pins which can come loose. With this type of construction, wear is reduced to a negligible amount, and adjustment of wrist pin and crank pin bearings is unnecessary.

Main Bearings: Main bearings are of the ball type and are securely held in position by spacers. This type of bearing entirely eliminates the necessity of frequent adjustment or attention. The crank shaft is always in perfect alignment.

Crank Shaft: The crank shaft is a one-piece heat-treated forging of best quality open-hearth steel, of rugged design and of sufficient size to transmit the motor power and any additional stresses which may occur in service. Each crank shaft is counter-balanced (dynamically balanced to reduce vibration to a minimum, and is accurately machined to properly receive the ball-bearing races, crank pin bushing, flexible coupling, and centrifugal governor. Suitable provision is made to insure proper lubrication of all crank shaft bearings and bushings with the minimum amount of attention.

Coupling: Compressor and motor shafts are connected through a Morse Chain Company all-metal enclosed flexible coupling. This coupling consists of two sprockets, one mounted on, and keyed to, each shaft; the sprockets are wrapped by a single Morse Chain, the entire assembly being enclosed in a split aluminum grease-packed cover.

1. The crank pin of the connecting rod is fitted with a renewable bushing made of 1.____
   A. solid bronze   B. steel
   C. a lightweight casting   D. ball bearings

2. When the connecting rod is of the one-piece type,
   A. the wrist pins require frequent adjustment
   B. the crank pins require frequent adjustment
   C. the cotter pins frequently will come loose
   D. wear is reduced to a negligible amount

3. The centrifugal governor is bolted directly to the
   A. compressor crank shaft   B. main bearing
   C. piston pin   D. muffler

4. The number of oil control rings required for each piston is
   A. one   B. two   C. three   D. four

5. The compressor and motor shafts are connected through a flexible coupling. These couplings are _____ to the shafts.
   A. keyed   B. brazed   C. soldered   D. press-fit

KEY (CORRECT ANSWERS)

1. B
2. D
3. A
4. B
5. A

TEST 6

DIRECTIONS: Questions 1 through 6 are to be answered on the basis of the following reading passage. *PRINT THE LETTER OF THE CORRECT ANSWER IN THE SPACE AT THE RIGHT.*

Perhaps the strongest argument the mass transit backer has is the advantage in efficiency that mass transit has over the automobile in the urban traffic picture. It has been estimated that given comparable location and construction conditions, the subway can carry four times as many passengers per hour and cost half as much to build as urban highways. Yet public apathy regarding the mass transportation movement in the 1960's resulted in the building of more roads. Planned to provide 42,000 miles of highways in the period from 1956-72, including 7,500 miles within cities, the Federal Highway System project is now about two-thirds completed. The Highway Trust Fund supplies 90 percent of the cost of the system, with state and local sources putting up the rest of the money. By contrast, a municipality as had to put up the bulk of the cost of a rapid transit system. Although the system and its Trust Fund have come under attack in the past few years from environmentalists and groups opposed to the continued building of urban freeways—considered to be the most expensive, destructive, and inefficient segments of the system—a move by them to get the Trust Fund transformed into a general transportation fund at the expiration of the present program in 1972 seems to be headed nowhere.

1. Given similar building conditions and locations, a city that builds a subway instead of a highway can expect to receive for each dollar spent _____ as much transport value.
   A. half   B. twice   C. four times   D. eight times

   1._____

2. The general attitude of the public in the past ten years toward the mass transportation movement has been
   A. favorable   B. indifferent   C. enthusiastic   D. unfriendly

   2._____

3. The number of miles of highways still to be completed in the Federal Highway System project is MOST NEARLY
   A. 2,500   B. 5,000   C. 14,000   D. 28,000

   3._____

4. What do certain groups who object to some features of the Federal Highway System program want to do with the Highway Trust Fund after 1972?
   A. Extend it in order to complete the project
   B. Change it so that the money can be used for all types of transportation
   C. End it even if the project is not completed
   D. Change it so that the money will be used only for urban freeways

   4._____

5. Which one of the following statements is a VALID conclusion based on the facts in the above passage?
   A. The advantage of greater efficiency is the only argument that supporters of the mass transportation movement can offer.
   B. It was easier for cities to build roads rather than mass transit systems in the last 15 years because of the large financial contribution made by the Federal Government.

   5._____

C. Mass transit systems cause as much congestion and air pollution in cities as automobiles.
D. In 1972, the Highway Trust Fund becomes a general transportation fund.

6. The MAIN idea or theme of the above passage is that the
   A. cost of the Federal Highway System is shared by the federal, state, and local governments
   B. public is against spending money for building mass transportation facilities in the cities
   C. cities would benefit more from expansion and improvement of their mass transit systems than from the building of more highways
   D. building of mass transportation facilities has been slowed by the Highway Trust Fund

KEY (CORRECT ANSWERS)

1. D
2. B
3. C
4. B
5. B
6. C

TEST 7

DIRECTIONS: Questions 1 through 5 are to be answered on the basis of the following reading passage. *PRINT THE LETTER OF THE CORRECT ANSWER IN THE SPACE AT THE RIGHT.*

The use of role-playing as a training technique was developed during the past decade by social scientists, particularly psychologists, who have been active in training experiments. Originally, this technique was applied by clinical psychologists who discovered that a patient appears to gain understanding of an emotionally disturbing situation when encouraged to act out roles in that situation. As applied in government and business organizations, the purpose of role-playing is to aid employees to understand certain work problems involving interpersonal relations and to enable observers to evaluate various reactions to them. Thus, for example, on the problem of handling grievances, two individuals from the group might be selected to act out extemporaneously the parts of subordinate and supervisor. When this situation is enacted by various pairs among the class and the techniques and results are discussed, the members of the group are presumed to reach conclusions about the most effective means of handling similar situations. Often the use or role reversal, where participants take parts different from their actual work roles, assists individuals to gain more insight into other people's problems and viewpoints. Although role-playing can be a rewarding training device, the trainer must be aware of his responsibilities. If this technique is to be successful, thorough briefing of both actors and observers as to the situation in question, the participants' roles, and what to look for, is essential.

1. The role-playing technique was FIRST used for the purpose of
   A. measuring the effectiveness of training programs
   B. training supervisors in business organizations
   C. treating emotionally disturbed patients
   D. handling employee grievances

   1.____

2. When role-playing is used in private business as a training device, the CHIEF aim is to
   A. develop better relations between supervisor and subordinate in the handling of grievances
   B. come up with a solution to a specific problem that has arisen
   C. determine the training needs of the group
   D. increase employee understanding of the human-relation factors in work situations

   2.____

3. From the above passage, it is MOST reasonable to conclude that when role-playing is used, it is preferable to have the roles acted out by
   A. only one set of actors
   B. no more than two sets of actors
   C. several different sets of actors
   D. the trainer or trainers of the group

   3.____

4. It can be inferred from the above passage that a limitation of role-playing as a training method is that
   A. many work situations do not lend themselves to role-play
   B. employees are not experienced enough as actors to play the roles realistically
   C. only trainers who have psychological training can use it successfully
   D. participants who are observing and not acting do not benefit from it

5. To obtain *good* results from the use of role-play in training, a trainer should give participants
   A. a minimum of information about the situation so that they can act spontaneously
   B. scripts which illustrate the best method for handling the situation
   C. a complete explanation of the problem and the roles to be acted out
   D. a summary of work problems which involve interpersonal relations

KEY (CORRECT ANSWERS)

1. C
2. D
3. C
4. A
5. C

PREPARING WRITTEN MATERIAL

PARAGRAPH REARRANGEMENT
COMMENTARY

The sentences that follow are in scrambled order. You are to rearrange them in proper order and indicate the letter choice containing the correct answer at the space at the right.

Each group of sentences in this section is actually a paragraph presented in scrambled order. Each sentence in the group has a place in that paragraph; no sentence is to be left out. You are to read each group of sentences and decide upon the best order in which to put the sentences so as to form a well-organized paragraph.

The questions in this section measure the ability to solve a problem when all the facts relevant to its solution are not given.

More specifically, certain positions of responsibility and authority require the employee to discover connection between events sometimes, apparently, unrelated. In order to do this, the employee will find it necessary to correctly infer that unspecified events have probably occurred or are likely to occur. This ability becomes especially important when action must be taken on incomplete information.

Accordingly, these questions require competitors to choose among several suggested alternatives, each of which presents a different sequential arrangement of the events. Competitors must choose the MOST logical of the suggested sequences.

In order to do so, they may be required to draw on general knowledge to infer missing concepts or events that are essential to sequencing the given events. Competitors should be careful to infer only what is essential to the sequence. The plausibility of the wrong alternatives will always require the inclusion of unlikely events or of additional chains of events which are NOT essential to sequencing the given events.

It's very important to remember that you are looking for the best of the four possible choices, and that the best choice of all may not even be one of the answers you're given to choose from.

There is no one right way to solve these problems. Many people have found it helpful to first write out the order of the sentences, as they would have arranged them, on their scrap paper before looking at the possible answers. If their optimum answer is there, this can save them some time. If it isn't, this method can still give insight into solving the problem. Others find it most helpful to just go through each of the possible choices, contrasting each as they go along. You should use whatever method feels comfortable and works for you.

While most of these types of questions are not that difficult, we've added a higher percentage of the difficult type, just to give you more practice. Usually there are only one or two questions on this section that contain such subtle distinctions that you're unable to answer confidently. And you then may find yourself stuck deciding between two possible choices, neither of which you're sure about.

EXAMINATION SECTION
TEST 1

DIRECTIONS: The following groups of sentences need to be arranged in an order that makes sense. Select the letter preceding the sequence that represents the BEST sentence order. *PRINT THE LETTER OF THE CORRECT ANSWER IN THE SPACE AT THE RIGHT.*

1. I. The keyboard was purposely designed to be a little awkward to slow typists down.
    II. The arrangement of letters on the keyboard of a typewriter was not designed for the convenience of the typist.
    III. Fortunately, no one is suggesting that a new keyboard be designed right away.
    IV. If one were, we would have to learn to type all over again.
    V. The reason was that the early machines were slower than the typists and would jam easily.
    The CORRECT answer is:
    A. I, III, IV, II, V
    B. II, V, I, IV, III
    C. V, I, II, III, IV
    D. II, I, V, III, IV

2. I. The majority of the new service jobs are part-time or low-paying.
    II. According to the U.S. Bureau of Labor Statistics, jobs in the service sector constitute 72% of all jobs in this country.
    III. If more and more workers receive less and less money, who will buy the goods and services needed to keep the economy going?
    IV. The service sector is by far the fastest growing part of the United States economy.
    V. Some economists look upon this trend with great concern.
    The CORRECT answer is:
    A. II, IV, I, V, III
    B. II, III, IV, I, V
    C. V, IV, II, III, I
    D. III, I, II, IV, V

3. I. They can also affect one's endurance.
    II. This can stabilize blood sugar levels, and ensure that the brain is receiving a steady, constant, supply of glucose, so that one is *hitting on all cylinders* while taking the test.
    III. By food, we mean real food, not junk food or unhealthy snacks.
    IV. For this reason, it is important not to skip a meal, and to bring food with you to the exam.
    V. One's blood sugar levels can affect how clearly one is able to think and concentrate during an exam.
    The CORRECT answer is:
    A. V, IV, II, III, I
    B. V, II, I, IV, III
    C. V, I, IV, III, II
    D. V, IV, I, III, II

141

4. I. Those who are the embodiment of desire are absorbed in material quests, and those who are the embodiment of feeling are warriors who value power more than possession.
    II. These qualities are in everyone, but in different degrees.
    III. But those who value understanding yearn not for goods or victory, but for knowledge.
    IV. According to Plato, human behavior flows from three main sources: desire, emotion, and knowledge.
    V. In the perfect state, the industrial forces would produce but not rule, the military would protect but not rule, and the forces of knowledge, the philosopher kings, would reign.
    The CORRECT answer is:
    A. IV, V, I, II, III
    B. V, I, II, III, IV
    C. IV, III, II, I, V
    D. IV, II, I, III, V

5. I. Of the more than 26,000 tons of garbage produced daily in New York City, 12,000 tons arrive daily at Fresh Kills.
    II. In a month, enough garbage accumulates there to fill the Empire State Building.
    III. In 1937, the Supreme Court halted the practice of dumping the trash of New York City into the sea.
    IV. Although the garbage is compacted, in a few years the mounds of garbage at Fresh Kills will be the highest points south of Maine's Mount Desert Island on the Eastern Seaboard.
    V. Instead, tugboats now pull barges of much of the trash to Staten Island and the largest landfill in the world, Fresh Kills.
    The CORRECT answer is:
    A. III, V, IV, I, II
    B. III, V, II, IV, I
    C. III, V, I, II, IV
    D. III, II, V, IV, I

6. I. Communists rank equality very high, but freedom very low.
    II. Unlike communists, conservatives place a high value on freedom and a very low value on equality.
    III. A recent study demonstrated that one way to classify people's political beliefs is to look at the importance placed on two words: freedom and equality.
    IV. Thus, by demonstrating how members of these groups feel about the two words, the study has proved to be useful for political analysts in several European countries.
    V. According to the study, socialists and liberals rank both freedom and equality very high, while fascists rate both very low.
    The CORRECT answer is:
    A. III, V, I, II, IV
    B. V, IV, III, I, II
    C. III, V, IV, II, I
    D. III, I, II, IV, V

7. I. "Can there be anything more amazing than this?"
    II. If the riddle is successfully answered, his dead brothers will be brought back to life.
    III. "Even though man sees those around him dying every day," says Dharmaraj, "he still believes and acts as if he were immortal."
    IV. "What is the cause of ceaseless wonder?" asks the Lord of the Lake.
    V. In the ancient epic, The Mahabharata, a riddle is asked of one of the Pandava brothers.
    The CORRECT answer is:
    A. V, II, I, IV, III
    B. V, IV, III, I, II
    C. V, II, IV, III, I
    D. V, II, IV, I, III

8. I. On the contrary, the two main theories—the cooperative (neoclassical) theory and the radical (labor theory)—clearly rest on very different assumptions, which have very different ethical overtones.
    II. The distribution of income is the primary factor in determining the relative levels of material well-being that different groups or individuals attain.
    III. Of all issues in economics, the distribution of income is one of the most controversial.
    IV. The neoclassical theory tends to support the existing income distribution (or minor changes), while the labor theory ends to support substantial changes in the way income is distributed.
    V. The intensity of the controversy reflects the fact that different economic theories are not purely neutral, *detached* theories with no ethical or moral implications.
    The CORRECT answer is:
    A. II, I, V, IV, III
    B. III, II, V, I, IV
    C. III, V, II, I, IV
    D. III, V, IV, I, II

9. I. The pool acts as a broker and ensures that the cheapest power gets used first.
    II. Every six seconds, the pool's computer monitors all of the generating stations in the state and decides which to ask for more power and which to cut back.
    III. The buying and selling of electrical power is handled by the New York Power Pool in Guilderland, New York.
    IV. This is to the advantage of both the buying and selling utilities.
    V. The pool began operation in 1970, and consists of the state's eight electric utilities.
    The CORRECT answer is:
    A. V, I, II, III, IV
    B. IV, II, I, III, V
    C. III, V, I, IV, II
    D. V, III, IV, II, I

10. I. Modern English is much simpler grammatically than Old English.
    II. Finnish grammar is very complicated; there are some fifteen cases, for example.
    III. Chinese, a very old language, may seem to be the exception, but it is the great number of characters/words that must be mastered that makes it so difficult to learn, not its grammar.
    IV. The newest literary language—that is, written as well as spoken—is Finish, whose literary roots go back only to about the middle of the nineteenth century.
    V. Contrary to popular belief, the longer a language is been in use the simpler its grammar—not the reverse.

    The CORRECT answer is:
    A. IV, I, II, III, V
    B. V, I, IV, II, III
    C. I, II, IV, III, V
    D. IV, II, III, I, V

10.____

KEY (CORRECT ANSWERS)

1.	D	6.	A
2.	A	7.	C
3.	C	8.	B
4.	D	9.	C
5.	C	10.	B

TEST 2

DIRECTIONS: This type of question tests your ability to recognize accurate paraphrasing, well-constructed paragraphs, and appropriate style and tone. It is important that the answer you select contains only the facts or concepts given in the original sentences. It is also important that you be aware of incomplete sentences, inappropriate transitions, unsupported opinions, incorrect usage, and illogical sentence order. Paragraphs that do not include all the necessary facts and concepts, that distort them, or that add new ones are not considered correct.

The format for this section may vary. Sometimes, long paragraphs are given, and emphasis is placed on style and organization. Our first five questions are of this type. Other times, the paragraphs are shorter, and there is less emphasis on style and more emphasis on accurate representation of information. Our second group of five questions are of this nature.

For each of Questions 1 through 10, select the paragraph that BEST expresses the ideas contained in the sentences above it. *PRINT THE LETTER OF THE CORRECT ANSWER IN THE SPACE AT THE RIGHT.*

1. I. Listening skills are very important for managers.
   II. Listening skills are not usually emphasized.
   III. Whenever managers are depicted in books, manuals or the media, they are always talking, never listening.
   IV. We'd like you to read the enclosed handout on listening skills and to try to consciously apply them this week.
   V. We guarantee they will improve the quality of your interactions.

   A. Unfortunately, listening skills are not usually emphasized for managers. Managers are always depicted as talking, never listening. We'd like you to read the enclosed handout on listening skills. Please try to apply these principles this week. If you do, we guarantee they will improve the quality of your interactions.
   B. The enclosed handout on listening skills will be important improving the quality of your interactions. We guarantee it. All you have to do is take sometime this week to read and to consciously try to apply the principles. Listening skills are very important for manages, but they are not usually emphasized. Whenever managers are depicted in books, manuals or the media, they are always talking, never listening.
   C. Listening well is one of the most important skills a manager can have, yet it's not usually given much attention. Think about any representation of managers in books, manuals, or in the media that you may have seen. They're always talking, never listening. We'd like you to read the enclosed handout on listening skills and consciously try to apply them the rest of the week. We guarantee you will see a difference in the quality of your interactions.

1._____

145

D. Effective listening, one very important tool in the effective manager's arsenal, is usually not emphasized enough. The usual depiction of managers in books, manuals or the media is one in which they are always talking, never listening. We'd like you to read the enclosed handout and consciously try to apply the information contained therein throughout the rest of the week. We feel sure that you will see a marked difference in the quality of your interactions.

2.
I. Chekhov wrote three dramatic masterpieces which share certain themes and formats: Uncle Vanya, The Cherry Orchard, and The Three Sisters.
II. They are primarily concerned with the passage of time and how this erodes human aspirations.
III. The plays are haunted by the ghosts of the wasted life.
IV. The characters are concerned with life's lesser problems; however, such as the inability to make decisions, loyalty to the wrong cause, and the inability to be clear.
V. This results in sweet, almost aching, type of a sadness referred to as Chekhovian.

2.____

A. Chekhov wrote three dramatic masterpieces: Uncle Vanya, The Cherry Orchard, and The Three Sisters. These masterpieces share certain themes and formats: the passage of time, how time erodes human aspirations, and the ghosts of wasted life. Each masterpiece is characterized by a sweet, almost aching, type of sadness that has become known as Chekhovian. The sweetness of this sadness hinges on the fact that it is not the great tragedies of life which are destroying these characters, but their minor flaws: indecisiveness, misplaced loyalty, unclarity.

B. The Cherry Orchard, Uncle Vanya, and The Three Sisters are three dramatic masterpieces written by Chekhov that use similar formats to explore a common theme. Each is primarily concerned with the way that passing time wears down human aspirations, and each is haunted by the ghosts of the wasted life. The characters are shown struggling futilely with the lesser problems of life: indecisiveness, loyalty to the wrong cause, and the inability to be clear. These struggles create a mood of sweet, almost aching, sadness that has become known as Chekhovian.

C. Chekhov's dramatic masterpieces are, along with The Cherry Orchard, Uncle Vanya, and The Three Sisters. These plays share certain thematic and formal similarities. They are concerned most of all with the passage of time and the way in which time erodes human aspirations. Each play is haunted by the specter of the wasted life. Chekhov's characters are caught, however, by life's lesser snares: indecisiveness, loyalty to the wrong cause, and unclarity. The characteristic mood is a sweet, almost aching type of sadness that has come to be known as Chekhovian.

D. A Chekhovian mood is characterized by sweet, almost aching, sadness. The term comes from three dramatic tragedies by Chekhov which revolve around the sadness of a wasted life. The three masterpieces (Uncle Vanya, The Three Sisters, and The Cherry Orchard) share the same theme and format. The plays are concerned with how the passage of time erodes human aspirations. They are peopled with characters who are struggling with life's lesser problems. These are people who are indecisive, loyal to the wrong causes, or are unable to make themselves clear.

3.
  I. Movie previews have often helped producers decide which parts of movies they should take out or leave in.
  II. The first 1933 preview of King Kong was very helpful to the producers because many people ran screaming from the theater and would not return when four men first attacked by Kong were eaten by giant spiders.
  III. The 1950 premiere of Sunset Boulevard resulted in the filming of an entirely new beginning, and a delay of six months in the film's release.
  IV. In the original opening scene, William Holden was in a morgue talking with thirty-six other "corpses" about the ways some of them had died.
  V. When he began to tell them of his life with Gloria Swanson, the audience found this hilarious, instead of taking the scene seriously.

    A. Movie previews have often helped producers decide what parts of movies they should leave in or take out. For example, the first preview of King Kong in 1933 was very helpful. In one scene, four men were first attacked by Kong and then eaten by giant spiders. Many members of the audience ran screaming from the theater and would not return. The premiere of the 1950 film Sunset Boulevard was also very helpful. In the original opening scene, William Holden was in a morgue with thirty-six other "corpses," discussing the ways some of them had died. When he began to tell them of his life with Gloria Swanson, the audience found this hilarious. They were supposed to take the scene seriously. The result was a delay of six months in the release of the film while a new beginning was added.
    B. Movie previews have often helped producers decide whether they should change various parts of a movie. After the 1933 preview of King Kong, a scene in which four men who had been attacked by Kong were eaten by giant spiders was taken out as many people ran screaming from the theater and would not return. The 1950 premiere of Sunset Boulevard also led to some changes. In the original opening scene, William Holden was in a morgue talking with thirty-six other "corpses" about the ways some of them had died. When he began to tell them of his life with Gloria Swanson, the audience found this hilarious, instead of taking the scene seriously.
    C. What do Sunset Boulevard and King Kong have in common? Both show the value of using movie previews to test audience reaction. The first 1933 preview of King Kong showed that a scene showing four men being eaten by giant spiders after having been attacked by Kong was too frightening for many people. They ran screaming from the theater and couldn't be coaxed back. The 1950 premiere of Sunset Boulevard was also a scream, but not the kind the producers intended. The movie opens

3._____

with William Holden lying in a morgue discussing the ways they had died with thirty-six other "corpses." When he began to tell them of his life with Gloria Swanson, the audience couldn't take him seriously. Their laughter caused a six-month delay while the beginning was rewritten.

D. Producers very often use movie previews to decide if changes are needed. The premiere of Sunset Boulevard in 1950 led to a new beginning and a six-month delay in film release. At the beginning, William Holden and thirty-six other "corpses" discuss the ways some of them died. Rather than taking this seriously, the audience thought it was hilarious when he began to tell them of his life with Gloria Swanson. The first 1933 preview of King Kong was very helpful for its producers because one scene so terrified the audience that many of them ran screaming from the theater and would not return. In this particular scene, four men who had first been attacked by Kong were eaten by giant spiders.

4. I. It is common for supervisors to view employees as "things" to be manipulated. 4.____
    II. This approach does not motivate employees, nor does the carrot-and-stick approach because employees often recognize these behaviors and resent them.
    III. Supervisors can change these behaviors by using self-inquiry and persistence.
    IV. The best managers genuinely respect those they work with, are supportive and helpful, and are interested in working as a team with those they supervise.
    V. They disagree with the Golden Rule that says "he or she who has the gold makes the rules."

    A. Some managers act as if they think the Golden Rule means "he or she who has the gold makes the rules." They show disrespect to employees by seeing them as "things" to be manipulated. Obviously, this approach does not motivate employees any more than the carrot-and-stick approach motivates them. The employees are smart enough to spot these behaviors and resent them. On the other hand, the managers genuinely respect those they work with, are supportive and helpful, and are interested in working as a team. Self-inquiry and persistence can change even the former type of supervisor into the latter.
    B. Many supervisors all into the trap of viewing employees as "things" to be manipulated, or try to motivate them by using a carrot-and-stick approach. These methods do not motivate employees, who often recognize the behaviors and resent them. Supervisors can change these behaviors, however, by using self-inquiry and persistence. The best managers are supportive and helpful, and have genuine respect for those with whom they work. They are interested in working as a team with those they supervise. To them, the Golden Rule is not "he or she who has the gold makes the rules."
    C. Some supervisors see employees as "things" to be used or manipulated using a carrot-and-stick technique. These methods don't work. Employees often see through them and resent them. A supervisor who

wants to change may do so. The techniques of self-inquiry and persistence can be used to turn him or her into the type of supervisor who doesn't think the Golden Rule is "he or she who has the gold makes the rules." They may become like the best managers who treat those with whom they work with respect and give them help and support. These are the manager who know how to build a team.

D. Unfortunately, many supervisors act as if their employees are objects whose movements they can position at will. This mistaken belief has the same result as another popular motivational technique—the carrot-and-stick approach. Both attitudes can lead to the same result—resentment from those employees who recognize the behaviors for what they are. Supervisors who recognize these behaviors can change through the use of persistence and the use of self-inquiry. It's important to remember that the best managers respect their employees. They readily give necessary help and support and are interested in working as a team with those they supervise. To these managers, the Golden Rule is not "he or she who has the gold makes the rules."

5.
I. The first half of the nineteenth century produced a group of pessimistic poets—Byron, De Musset, Heine, Pushkin, and Leopardi.
II. It also produced a group of pessimistic composers—Schubert, Chopin, Schumann, and even the later Beethoven.
III. Above all, in philosophy, there was the profoundly pessimistic philosopher, Schopenhauer.
IV. The Revolution was dead, the Bourbons were restored, the feudal barons were reclaiming their land, and progress everywhere was being suppressed, as the great age was over.
V. "I thank God," said Goethe, "that I am not young in so thoroughly finished a world."

5._____

  A. "I thank God," said Goethe, "that I am not young in so thoroughly finished a world." The Revolution was dead, the Bourbons were restored, the feudal barons were reclaiming their land, and progress everywhere was being suppressed. The first half of the nineteenth century produced a group of pessimistic poets: Byron, De Musset, Heine, Pushkin, and Leopardi. It also produced pessimistic composers: Schubert, Chopin, Schumann. Although Beethoven came later, he fits into this group, too. Finally and above all, it also produced a profoundly pessimistic philosopher, Schopenhauer. The great age was over.
  B. The first half of the nineteenth century produced a group of pessimistic poets: Byron, De Musset, Heine, Pushkin, and Leopardi. It produced a group of pessimistic composers: Schubert, Chopin, Schumann, and even the later Beethoven. Above all, it produced a profoundly pessimistic philosopher, Schopenhauer. For each of these men, the great age was over. The Revolution was dead, and the Bourbons were restored. The feudal barons were reclaiming their land, and progress everywhere was being suppressed.

C. The great age was over. The Revolution was dead—the Bourbons were restored, and the feudal barons were reclaiming their land. Progress everywhere was being suppressed. Out of this climate came a profound pessimism. Poets, like Byron, De Musset, Heine, Pushkin, and Leopardi; composers, like Schubert, Chopin, Schumann, and even the later Beethoven; and above all, a profoundly pessimistic philosopher, Schopenauer. This pessimism which arose in the first half of the nineteenth century is illustrated by these words of Goethe, "I thank God that I am not young in so thoroughly finished a world."

D. The first half of the nineteenth century produced a group of pessimistic poets, Byron, De Musset, Heine, Pushkin, and Leopardi—and a group of pessimistic composers, Schubert, Chopin, Schumann, and the later Beethoven. Above it all, it produced a profoundly pessimistic philosopher, Schopenhauer. The great age was over. The Revolution was dead, the Bourbons were restored, the feudal barons were reclaiming their land, and progress everywhere was being suppressed. "I thank God," said Goethe, "that I am not young in so thoroughly finished a world."

6. I. A new manager sometimes may feel insecure about his or her competence in the new position.
    II. The new manager may then exhibit defensive or arrogant behavior towards those one supervises, or the new manager may direct overly flattering behavior toward one's new supervisor.

    A. Sometimes, a new manager may feel insecure about his or her ability to perform well in this new position. The insecurity may lead him or her to treat others differently. He or she may display arrogant or defensive behavior towards those he or she supervises, or be overly flattering to his or her new supervisor.
    B. A new manager may sometimes feel insecure about his or her ability to perform well in the new position. He or she may then become arrogant, defensive, or overly flattering towards those he or she works with.
    C. There are times when a new manager may be insecure about how well he or she can perform in the new job. The new manager may also behave defensive or act in an arrogant way towards those he or she supervises, or overly flatter his or her boss.
    D. Sometimes a new manager may feel insecure about his or her ability to perform well in the new position. He or she may then display arrogant or defensive behavior towards those they supervise, or become overly flattering towards their supervisors.

6._____

7. I. It is possible to eliminate unwanted behavior by bringing it under stimulus control—tying the behavior to a cue, and then never, or rarely, giving the cue.
    II. One trainer successfully used this method to keep an energetic young porpoise from coming out of her tank whenever she felt like it, which was potentially dangerous.
    III. Her trainer taught her to do it for a reward, in response to a hand signal, and then rarely gave the signal.

7._____

A. Unwanted behavior can be eliminated by tying the behavior to a cue, and then never, or rarely, giving the cue. This is called stimulus control. One trainer was able to use this method to keep an energetic young porpoise from coming out of her tank by teaching her to come out for a reward in response to a hand signal, and then rarely giving the signal.
B. Stimulus control can be used to eliminate unwanted behavior. In this method, behavior is tied to a cue, and then the cue is rarely, if ever, given. One trainer was able to successfully use stimulus control to keep an energetic young porpoise from coming out of her tank whenever she felt like it—a potentially dangerous practice. She taught the porpoise to come out for a reward when she gave a hand signal, and then rarely gave the signal.
C. It is possible to eliminate behavior that is undesirable by bringing it under stimulus control by tying behavior to a signal, and then rarely giving the signal. One trainer successfully used this method to keep an energetic porpoise from coming out of her tank, a potentially dangerous situation. Her trainer taught the porpoise to do it for a reward, in response to a hand signal, and then would rarely give the signal.
D. By using stimulus control, it is possible to eliminate unwanted behavior by tying the behavior to a cue, and then rarely or never give the cue. One trainer was able to use this method to successfully stop a young porpoise from coming out of her tank whenever she felt like it. To curb this potentially dangerous practice, the porpoise was taught by the trainer to come out of the tank for a reward, in response to a hand signal, and then rarely given the signal.

8. I. There is a great deal of concern over the safety of commercial trucks, caused by their greatly increased role in serious accidents since federal deregulation in 1981.
    II. Recently, 60 percent of trucks in New York and Connecticut and 70 percent of trucks in Maryland randomly stopped by state troopers failed safety inspections.
    III. Sixteen states in the United States require no training at all for truck drivers.

    A. Since federal deregulation in 1981, there has been a great deal of concern over the safety of commercial trucks, and their greatly increased role in serious accidents. Recently, 60 percent of trucks in New York and Connecticut, and 70 percent of trucks in Maryland failed safety inspections. Sixteen states in the United States require no training at all for truck drivers.
    B. There is a great deal of concern over the safety of commercial trucks since federal deregulation in 1981. Their role in serious accidents has greatly increased. Recently, 60 percent of trucks randomly stopped in Connecticut and New York and 70 percent in Maryland failed safety inspections conducted by state troopers. Sixteen states in the United States provide no training at all for truck drivers.
    C. Commercial trucks have a greatly increased role in serious accidents since federal deregulation in 1981. This has led to a great deal of concern.

8.____

Recently, 70 percent of trucks in Maryland and 60 percent of trucks in New York and Connecticut failed inspection of those that were randomly stopped by state troopers. Sixteen states in the United States require no training for all truck drivers.

D. Since federal deregulation in 1981, the role that commercial trucks have played in serious accidents has greatly increased, and this has led to a great deal of concern. Recently, 60 percent of trucks in New York and Connecticut, and 70 percent of trucks in Maryland randomly stopped by state troopers failed safety inspections. Sixteen states in the U.S. don't require any training for truck drivers.

9.
I. No matter how much some people have, they still feel unsatisfied and want more, or want to keep what they have forever.
II. One recent television documentary showed several people flying from New York to Paris for a one-day shopping spree to buy platinum earrings, because they were bored.
III. In Brazil, some people were ordering coffins that cost a minimum of $45,000 and are equipping them with deluxe stereos, televisions, and other graveyard necessities.

9._____

A. Some people, despite having a great deal, still feel unsatisfied and want more, or think they can keep what they have forever. One recent documentary on television showed several people enroute from Paris to New York for a one day shopping spree to buy platinum earrings, because they were bored. Some people in Brazil are even ordering coffins equipped with such graveyard necessities as deluxe stereos and televisions. The price of the coffins start at $45,000.
B. No matter how much some people have, they may feel unsatisfied. This leads them to want more, or to want to keep what they have forever. Recently, a television documentary depicting several people flying from New York to Paris for a one day shopping spree to buy platinum earrings. They were bored. Some people in Brazil are ordering coffins that cost at least $45,000 and come equipped with deluxe televisions, stereos and other necessary graveyard items.
C. Some people will be dissatisfied no matter how much they have. They may want more, or they may want to keep what they have forever. One recent television documentary showed several people, motivated by boredom, jetting from New York to Paris for a one-day shopping spree to buy platinum earrings. In Brazil, some people are ordering coffins equipped with deluxe stereos, televisions and other graveyard necessities. The minimum price for these coffins—$45,000.
D. Some people are never satisfied. No matter how much they have they still want more, or think they can keep what they have forever. One television documentary recently showed several people flying from New York to Paris for the day to buy platinum earrings because they were bored. In Brazil, some people are ordering coffins that cost $45,000 and are equipped with deluxe stereos, televisions and other graveyard necessities.

10. I. A television signal or video signal has three parts.
    II. Its parts are the black-and-white portion, the color portion, and the synchronizing (sync) pulses, which keep the picture stable.
    III. Each video source, whether it's a camera or a video-cassette recorder contains its own generator of these synchronizing pulses to accompany the picture that it's sending in order to keep it steady and straight.
    IV. In order to produce a clean recording, a video-cassette recorder must "lock-up" to the sync pulses that are part of the video it is trying to record, and this effort may be very noticeable if the device does not have gunlock.

    A. There are three parts to a television or video signal: the black-and-white part, the color part, and the synchronizing (sync) pulses, which keep the picture stable. Whether it's a video-cassette recorder or a camera, each video source contains its own pulse that synchronizes and generates the picture it's sending in order to keep it straight and steady. A video-cassette recorder must "lock up" to the sync pulses that are part of the video it's trying to record. If the device doesn't have gunlock, this effort must be very noticeable.
    B. A video signal or television is comprised of three parts: the black-and-white portion, the color portion, and the sync (synchronizing) pulses, which keep the picture stable. Whether it's a camera or a video-cassette recorder, each video source contains its own generator of these synchronizing pulses. These accompany the picture that it's sending in order to keep it straight and steady. A video-cassette recorder must "lock up" to the sync pulses that are part of the video it is trying to record in order to produce a clean recording. This effort may be very noticeable if the device does not have gunlock.
    C. There are three parts to a television or video signal: the color portion, the black-and-white portion, and the sync (synchronizing pulses). These keep the picture stable. Each video source, whether it's a video-cassette recorder or a camera, generates these synchronizing pulses accompanying the picture it's sending in order to keep it straight and steady. If a clean recording is to be produced, a video-cassette recorder must store the sync pulses that are part of the video it is trying to record. This effort may not be noticeable if the device does not have gunlock.
    D. A television signal or video signal has three parts—the black-and-white portion, the color portion, and the synchronizing (sync) pulses. It's the sync pulses which keep the picture stable, which accompany it and keep it steady and straight. Whether it's a camera or a video-cassette recorder, each video source contains its own generator of these synchronizing pulses. To produce a clean recording, a video-cassette recorder must "lock up" to the sync pulses that are part of the video it is trying to record. If the device does not have gunlock, this effort may be very noticeable.

KEY (CORRECT ANSWERS)

1. C
2. B
3. A
4. B
5. D
6. A
7. B
8. D
9. C
10. D

PREPARING WRITTEN MATERIAL
EXAMINATION SECTION
TEST 1

DIRECTIONS: Each of the sentences in this test may be classified under one of the following four categories:
  A. Faulty because of incorrect grammar or word usage
  B. Faulty because of incorrect punctuation
  C. Faulty because of incorrect capitalization or incorrect spelling
  D. Correct

Examine each sentence carefully to determine under which of the above four options it is best classified. Then, in the space to the right, print the capital letter preceding the option which is the BEST of the four suggested above. (Note that each faulty sentence contains but one type of error. Consider a sentence to be correct if it contains none of the types of errors mentioned, even though there may be other correct ways of expressing the same thought.)

1. He sent the notice to the clerk who you hired yesterday. 1.____
2. It must be admitted, however that you were not informed of this change. 2.____
3. Only the employee who have served in this grade for at least two years are eligible for promotion. 3.____
4. The work was divided equally between she and Mary. 4.____
5. He thought that you were not available at that time. 5.____
6. When the messenger returns; please give him this package. 6.____
7. The new secretary prepared, typed, addressed, and delivered, the notices. 7.____
8. Walking into the room, his desk can be seen at the rear. 8.____
9. Although John has worked here longer than She, he produces a smaller amount of work. 9.____
10. She said she could of typed this report yesterday. 10.____
11. Neither one of these procedures are adequate for the efficient performance of this task. 11.____
12. The typewriter is the tool of the typist; the cash register, the tool of the cashier. 12.____

13. "The assignment must be completed as soon as possible" said the supervisor.   13.____

14. As you know, office handbooks are issued to all new Employees.   14.____

15. Writing a speech is sometimes easier than to deliver it before an audience.   15.____

16. Mr. Brown our accountant, will audit the accounts next week.   16.____

17. Give the assignment to whomever is able to do it most efficiently.   17.____

18. The supervisor expected either your or I to file these reports.   18.____

KEY (CORRECT ANSWERS)

1.	A	11.	A
2.	B	12.	C
3.	D	13.	B
4.	A	14.	C
5.	D	15.	A
6.	B	16.	B
7.	B	17.	A
8.	A	18.	A
9.	C		
10.	A		

TEST 2

DIRECTIONS: Each of the sentences in this test may be classified under one of the following four categories:
- A. Faulty because of incorrect grammar or word usage
- B. Faulty because of incorrect punctuation
- C. Faulty because of incorrect capitalization or incorrect spelling
- D. Correct

Examine each sentence carefully to determine under which of the above four options it is best classified. Then, in the space to the right, print the capital letter preceding the option which is the BEST of the four suggested above. (Note that each faulty sentence contains but one type of error. Consider a sentence to be correct if it contains none of the types of errors mentioned, even though there may be other correct ways of expressing the same thought.)

1. The fire apparently started in the storeroom, which is usually locked. 1.____
2. On approaching the victim, two bruises were noticed by this officer. 2.____
3. The officer, who was there examined the report with great care. 3.____
4. Each employee in the office had a seperate desk. 4.____
5. All employees including members of the clerical staff, were invited to the lecture. 5.____
6. The suggested Procedure is similar to the one now in use. 6.____
7. No one was more pleased with the new procedure than the chauffeur. 7.____
8. He tried to persaude her to change the procedure. 8.____
9. The total of the expenses charged to petty cash were high. 9.____
10. An understanding between him and I was finally reached. 10.____

KEY (CORRECT ANSWERS)

1.	D	6.	C
2.	A	7.	D
3.	B	8.	C
4.	C	9.	A
5.	B	10.	A

TEST 3

DIRECTIONS: Each of the sentences in this test may be classified under one of the following four categories:
   A. Faulty because of incorrect grammar or word usage
   B. Faulty because of incorrect punctuation
   C. Faulty because of incorrect capitalization or incorrect spelling
   D. Correct

Examine each sentence carefully to determine under which of the above four options it is best classified. Then, in the space to the right, print the capital letter preceding the option which is the BEST of the four suggested above. (Note that each faulty sentence contains but one type of error. Consider a sentence to be correct if it contains none of the types of errors mentioned, even though there may be other correct ways of expressing the same thought.)

1. They told both he and I that the prisoner had escaped. 1.____

2. Any superior officer, who, disregards the just complaint of his subordinates, is remiss in the performance of his duty. 2.____

3. Only those members of the national organization who resided in the Middle West attended the conference in Chicago. 3.____

4. We told him to give the national organization assignment to whoever was available. 4.____

5. Please do not disappoint and embarass us by not appearing in court. 5.____

6. Although the office's speech proved to be entertaining, the topic was not relevent to the main theme of the conference. 6.____

7. In February all new officers attended a training course in which they were learned in their principal duties and the fundamental operating procedure of the department. 7.____

8. I personally seen inmate Jones threaten inmates Smith and Green with bodily harm if they refused to participate in the plot. 8.____

9. To the layman, who on a chance visit to the prison observes everything functioning smoothly, the maintenance of prison discipline may seem to be a relatively easily realizable objective. 9.____

10. The prisoners in cell block fourty were forbidden to sit on the cell cots during the recreation hour. 10.____

KEY (CORRECT ANSWERS)

1.	A	6.	C
2.	B	7.	A
3.	C	8.	A
4.	D	9.	D
5.	C	10.	C

TEST 4

DIRECTIONS: Each of the sentences in this test may be classified under one of the following four categories:
- A. Faulty because of incorrect grammar or word usage
- B. Faulty because of incorrect punctuation
- C. Faulty because of incorrect capitalization or incorrect spelling
- D. Correct

Examine each sentence carefully to determine under which of the above four options it is best classified. Then, in the space to the right, print the capital letter preceding the option which is the BEST of the four suggested above. (Note that each faulty sentence contains but one type of error. Consider a sentence to be correct if it contains none of the types of errors mentioned, even though there may be other correct ways of expressing the same thought.)

1. I cannot encourage you any. 1.____
2. You always look well in those sort of clothes. 2.____
3. Shall we go to the park? 3.____
4. The man whome he introduced was Mr. Carey. 4.____
5. She saw the letter laying here this morning. 5.____
6. It should rain before the Afternoon is over. 6.____
7. They have already went home. 7.____
8. That Jackson will be elected is evident. 8.____
9. He does not hardly approve of us. 9.____
10. It was he, who won the prize. 10.____

KEY (CORRECT ANSWERS)

1.	A	6.	C
2.	A	7.	A
3.	D	8.	D
4.	C	9.	A
5.	A	10.	B

TEST 5

DIRECTIONS: Each of the sentences in this test may be classified under one of the following four categories:
- A. Faulty because of incorrect grammar or word usage
- B. Faulty because of incorrect punctuation
- C. Faulty because of incorrect capitalization or incorrect spelling
- D. Correct

Examine each sentence carefully to determine under which of the above four options it is best classified. Then, in the space to the right, print the capital letter preceding the option which is the BEST of the four suggested above. (Note that each faulty sentence contains but one type of error. Consider a sentence to be correct if it contains none of the types of errors mentioned, even though there may be other correct ways of expressing the same thought.)

1. Shall we go to the park. 1.____
2. They are, alike, in this particular way. 2.____
3. They gave the poor man sume food when he knocked on the door. 3.____
4. I regret the loss caused by the error. 4.____
5. The students' will have a new teacher. 5.____
6. They sweared to bring out all the facts. 6.____
7. He decided to open a branch store on 33rd street. 7.____
8. His speed is equal and more than that of a racehorse. 8.____
9. He felt very warm on that Summer day. 9.____
10. He was assisted by his friend, who lives in the next house. 10.____

KEY (CORRECT ANSWERS)

1.	B	6.	A
2.	B	7.	C
3.	C	8.	A
4.	D	9.	C
5.	B	10.	D

TEST 6

DIRECTIONS: Each of the sentences in this test may be classified under one of the following four categories:
  A. Faulty because of incorrect grammar or word usage
  B. Faulty because of incorrect punctuation
  C. Faulty because of incorrect capitalization or incorrect spelling
  D. Correct

Examine each sentence carefully to determine under which of the above four options it is best classified. Then, in the space to the right, print the capital letter preceding the option which is the BEST of the four suggested above. (Note that each faulty sentence contains but one type of error. Consider a sentence to be correct if it contains none of the types of errors mentioned, even though there may be other correct ways of expressing the same thought.)

1. The climate of New York is colder than California. 1._____
2. I shall wait for you on the corner. 2._____
3. Did we see the boy who, we think, is the leader. 3._____
4. Being a modest person, John seldom talks about his invention. 4._____
5. The gang is called the smith street bos. 5._____
6. He seen the man break into the store. 6._____
7. We expected to lay still there for quite a while. 7._____
8. He is considered to be the Leader of his organization. 8._____
9. Although I recieved an invitation, I won't go. 9._____
10. The letter must be here some place. 10._____

KEY (CORRECT ANSWERS)

1. A   6. A
2. D   7. A
3. B   8. C
4. D   9. C
5. C   10. A

TEST 7

DIRECTIONS: Each of the sentences in this test may be classified under one of the following four categories:
- A. Faulty because of incorrect grammar or word usage
- B. Faulty because of incorrect punctuation
- C. Faulty because of incorrect capitalization or incorrect spelling
- D. Correct

Examine each sentence carefully to determine under which of the above four options it is best classified. Then, in the space to the right, print the capital letter preceding the option which is the BEST of the four suggested above. (Note that each faulty sentence contains but one type of error. Consider a sentence to be correct if it contains none of the types of errors mentioned, even though there may be other correct ways of expressing the same thought.)

1. I though it to be he. 1.____
2. We expect to remain here for a long time. 2.____
3. The committee was agreed. 3.____
4. Two-thirds of the building are finished. 4.____
5. The water was froze. 5.____
6. Everyone of the salesmen must supply their own car. 6.____
7. Who is the author of Gone With the Wind? 7.____
8. He marched on and declaring that he would never surrender. 8.____
9. Who shall I say called? 9.____
10. Everyone has left but they. 10.____

KEY (CORRECT ANSWERS)

1.	A	6.	A
2.	D	7.	B
3.	D	8.	A
4.	A	9.	D
5.	A	10.	D

TEST 8

DIRECTIONS: Each of the sentences in this test may be classified under one of the following four categories:
  A. Faulty because of incorrect grammar or word usage
  B. Faulty because of incorrect punctuation
  C. Faulty because of incorrect capitalization or incorrect spelling
  D. Correct

Examine each sentence carefully to determine under which of the above four options it is best classified. Then, in the space to the right, print the capital letter preceding the option which is the BEST of the four suggested above. (Note that each faulty sentence contains but one type of error. Consider a sentence to be correct if it contains none of the types of errors mentioned, even though there may be other correct ways of expressing the same thought.)

1. Who did we give the order to? 1._____
2. Send your order in immediately. 2._____
3. I believe I paid the Bill. 3._____
4. I have not met but one person. 4._____
5. Why aren't Tom, and Fred, going to the dance? 5._____
6. What reason is there for him not going? 6._____
7. The seige of Malta was a tremendous event. 7._____
8. I was there yesterday I assure you 8._____
9. Your ukulele is better than mine. 9._____
10. No one was there only Mary. 10._____

KEY (CORRECT ANSWERS)

1. A   6. A
2. D   7. C
3. C   8. B
4. A   9. C
5. B   10. A

TEST 9

DIRECTIONS: In each of the following groups of sentences, one of the four sentences is faulty in grammar, punctuation, or capitalization. Select the INCORRECT sentence in each case.

1.
   A. If you had stood at home and done your homework, you would not have failed in arithmetic.
   B. Her affected manner annoyed every member of the audience.
   C. How will the new law affect our income taxes?
   D. The plants were not affected by the long, cold winter, but they succumbed to the drought of summer.

   1._____

2.
   A. He is one of the most able men who have been in the Senate.
   B. It is he who is to blame for the lamentable mistake.
   C. Haven't you a helpful suggestion to make at this time?
   D. The money was robbed from the blind man's cup.

   2._____

3.
   A. The amount of children in this school is steadily increasing.
   B. After taking an apple from the table, she went out to play.
   C. He borrowed a dollar from me.
   D. I had hoped my brother would arrive before me.

   3._____

4.
   A. Whom do you think I hear from every week?
   B. Who do you think is the right man for the job?
   C. Who do you think I found in the room?
   D. He is the man whom we considered a good candidate for the presidency.

   4._____

5.
   A. Quietly the puppy laid down before the fireplace.
   B. You have made your bed; now lie in it.
   C. I was badly sunburned because I had lain too long in the sun.
   D. I laid the doll on the bed and left the room.

   5._____

KEY (CORRECT ANSWERS)

1. A
2. D
3. A
4. C
5. A

166

PHILOSOPHY, PRINCIPLES, PRACTICES, AND TECHNICS
OF
SUPERVISION, ADMINISTRATION, MANAGEMENT, AND ORGANIZATION

TABLE OF CONTENTS

	Page
MEANING OF SUPERVISION	1
THE OLD AND THE NEW SUPERVISION	1
THE EIGHT (8) BASIC PRINCIPLES OF THE NEW SUPERVISION	1
I. Principle of Responsibility	1
II. Principle of Authority	2
III. Principle of Self-Growth	2
IV. Principle of Individual Worth	2
V. Principle of Creative Leadership	2
VI. Principle of Success and Failure	2
VII. Principle of Science	3
VIII. Principle of Cooperation	3
WHAT IS ADMINISTRATION?	3
I. Practices Commonly Classed as "Supervisory"	3
II. Practices Commonly Classed as "Administrative"	3
III. Practices Commonly Classed as Both "Supervisory" and "Administrative"	4
RESPONSIBILITIES OF THE SUPERVISOR	4
COMPETENCIES OF THE SUPERVISOR	4
THE PROFESSIONAL SUPERVISOR-EMPLOYEE RELATIONSHIP	4
MINI-TEXT IN SUPERVISION, ADMINISTRATION, MANAGEMENT, AND ORGANIZATION	5
I. Brief Highlights	5
A. Levels of Management	6
B. What the Supervisor Must Learn	6
C. A Definition of Supervision	6
D. Elements of the Team Concept	6
E. Principles of Organization	6
F. The Four Important Parts of Every Job	7
G. Principles of Delegation	7
H. Principles of Effective Communications	7
I. Principles of Work Improvement	7
J. Areas of Job Improvement	7
K. Seven Key Points in Making Improvements	8

	L.	Corrective Techniques for Job Improvement	8
	M.	A Planning Checklist	8
	N.	Five Characteristics of Good Directions	9
	O.	Types of Directions	9
	P.	Controls	9
	Q.	Orienting the New Employee	9
	R.	Checklist for Orienting New Employees	9
	S.	Principles of Learning	10
	T.	Causes of Poor Performance	10
	U.	Four Major Steps in On-the-Job Instructions	10
	V.	Employees Want Five Things	10
	W.	Some Don'ts in Regard to Praise	11
	X.	How to Gain Your Workers' Confidence	11
	Y.	Sources of Employee Problems	11
	Z.	The Supervisor's Key to Discipline	11
	AA.	Five Important Processes of Management	12
	BB.	When the Supervisor Fails to Plan	12
	CC.	Fourteen General Principles of Management	12
	DD.	Change	12
II.	Brief Topical Summaries		13
	A.	Who/What is the Supervisor?	13
	B.	The Sociology of Work	13
	C.	Principles and Practices of Supervision	14
	D.	Dynamic Leadership	14
	E.	Processes for Solving Problems	15
	F.	Training for Results	15
	G.	Health, Safety, and Accident Prevention	16
	H.	Equal Employment Opportunity	16
	I.	Improving Communications	16
	J.	Self-Development	17
	K.	Teaching and Training	17
		1. The Teaching Process	17
		a. Preparation	17
		b. Presentation	18
		c. Summary	18
		d. Application	18
		e. Evaluation	18
		2. Teaching Methods	18
		a. Lecture	18
		b. Discussion	18
		c. Demonstration	19
		d. Performance	19
		e. Which Method to Use	19

PHILOSOPHY, PRINCIPLES, PRACTICES, AND TECHNICS
OF
SUPERVISION, ADMINISTRATION, MANAGEMENT, AND ORGANIZATION

MEANING OF SUPERVISION

The extension of the democratic philosophy has been accompanied by an extension in the scope of supervision. Modern leaders and supervisors no longer think of supervision in the narrow sense of being confined chiefly to visiting employees, supplying materials, or rating the staff. They regard supervision as being intimately related to all the concerned agencies of society, they speak of the supervisor's function in terms of "growth," rather than the "improvement" of employees.

This modern concept of supervision may be defined as follows: Supervision is leadership and the development of leadership within groups which are cooperatively engaged in inspection, research, training, guidance, and evaluation.

THE OLD AND THE NEW SUPERVISION

TRADITIONAL
1. Inspection
2. Focused on the employee
3. Visitation
4. Random and haphazard
5. Imposed and authoritarian
6. One person usually

MODERN
1. Study and analysis
2. Focused on aims, materials, methods, supervisors, employees, environment
3. Demonstrations, intervisitation, workshops, directed reading, bulletins, etc.
4. Definitely organized and planned (scientific)
5. Cooperative and democratic
6. Many persons involved (creative)

THE EIGHT (8) BASIC PRINCIPLES OF THE NEW SUPERVISION

I. Principle of Responsibility
   Authority to act and responsibility for acting must be joined.
   A. If you give responsibility, give authority.
   B. Define employee duties clearly.
   C. Protect employees from criticism by others.
   D. Recognize the rights as well as obligations of employees.
   E. Achieve the aims of a democratic society insofar as it is possible within the area of your work.
   F. Establish a situation favorable to training and learning.
   G. Accept ultimate responsibility for everything done in your section, unit, office, division, department.
   H. Good administration and good supervision are inseparable.

II. Principle of Authority
The success of the supervisor is measured by the extent to which the power of authority is not used.
- A. Exercise simplicity and informality in supervision
- B. Use the simplest machinery of supervision
- C. If it is good for the organization as a whole, it is probably justified.
- D. Seldom be arbitrary or authoritative.
- E. Do not base your work on the power of position or of personality.
- F. Permit and encourage the free expression of opinions.

III. Principle of Self-Growth
The success of the supervisor is measured by the extent to which, and the speed with which, he is no longer needed.
- A. Base criticism on principles, not on specifics.
- B. Point out higher activities to employees.
- C. Train for self-thinking by employees to meet new situations.
- D. Stimulate initiative, self-reliance, and individual responsibility
- E. Concentrate on stimulating the growth of employees rather than on removing defects.

IV. Principle of Individual Worth
Respect for the individual is a paramount consideration in supervision.
- A. Be human and sympathetic in dealing with employees.
- B. Don't nag about things to be done.
- C. Recognize the individual differences among employees and seek opportunities to permit best expression of each personality.

V. Principle of Creative Leadership
The best supervision is that which is not apparent to the employee.
- A. Stimulate, don't drive employees to creative action.
- B. Emphasize doing good things.
- C. Encourage employees to do what they do best.
- D. Do not be too greatly concerned with details of subject or method.
- E. Do not be concerned exclusively with immediate problems and activities.
- F. Reveal higher activities and make them both desired and maximally possible.
- G. Determine procedures in the light of each situation but see that these are derived from a sound basic philosophy.
- H. Aid, inspire, and lead so as to liberate the creative spirit latent in all good employees.

VI. Principle of Success and Failure
There are no unsuccessful employees, only unsuccessful supervisors who have failed to give proper leadership.
- A. Adapt suggestions to the capacities, attitudes, and prejudices of employees.
- B. Be gradual, be progressive, be persistent.
- C. Help the employee find the general principle; have the employee apply his own problem to the general principle.
- D. Give adequate appreciation for good work and honest effort.
- E. Anticipate employee difficulties and help to prevent them.
- F. Encourage employees to do the desirable things they will do anyway.
- G. Judge your supervision by the results it secures.

VII. Principle of Science
Successful supervision is scientific, objective, and experimental. It is based on facts, not on prejudices.
- A. Be cumulative in results.
- B. Never divorce your suggestions from the goals of training.
- C. Don't be impatient of results.
- D. Keep all matters on a professional, not a personal, level.
- E. Do not be concerned exclusively with immediate problems and activities.
- F. Use objective means of determining achievement and rating where possible.

VIII. Principle of Cooperation
Supervision is a cooperative enterprise between supervisor and employee.
- A. Begin with conditions as they are.
- B. Ask opinions of all involved when formulating policies.
- C. Organization is as good as its weakest link.
- D. Let employees help to determine policies and department programs.
- E. Be approachable and accessible—physically and mentally.
- F. Develop pleasant social relationships.

WHAT IS ADMINISTRATION

Administration is concerned with providing the environment, the material facilities, and the operational procedures that will promote the maximum growth and development of supervisors and employees. (Organization is an aspect and a concomitant of administration.)

There is no sharp line of demarcation between supervision and administration; these functions are intimately interrelated and, often, overlapping. They are complementary activities.

I. Practices Commonly Classed as "Supervisory"
- A. Conducting employees' conferences
- B. Visiting sections, units, offices, divisions, departments
- C. Arranging for demonstrations
- D. Examining plans
- E. Suggesting professional reading
- F. Interpreting bulletins
- G. Recommending in-service training courses
- H. Encouraging experimentation
- I. Appraising employee morale
- J. Providing for intervisitation

II. Practices Commonly Classified as "Administrative"
- A. Management of the office
- B. Arrangement of schedules for extra duties
- C. Assignment of rooms or areas
- D. Distribution of supplies
- E. Keeping records and reports
- F. Care of audio-visual materials
- G. Keeping inventory records
- H. Checking record cards and books

  I. Programming special activities
  J. Checking on the attendance and punctuality of employees

 III. Practices Commonly Classified as Both "Supervisory" and "Administrative"
  A. Program construction
  B. Testing or evaluating outcomes
  C. Personnel accounting
  D. Ordering instructional materials

RESPONSIBILITIES OF THE SUPERVISOR

A person employed in a supervisory capacity must constantly be able to improve his own efficiency and ability. He represent the employer to the employees and only continuous self-examination can make him a capable supervisor.

Leadership and training are the supervisor's responsibility. An efficient working unit is one in which the employees work with the supervisor. It is his job to bring out the best in his employees. He must always be relaxed, courteous, and calm in his association with his employees. Their feelings are important, and a harsh attitude does not develop the most efficient employees.

COMPETENCES OF THE SUPERVISOR

  I. Complete knowledge of the duties and responsibilities of his position.
  II. To be able to organize a job, plan ahead, and carry through.
  III. To have self-confidence and initiative.
  IV. To be able to handle the unexpected situation and make quick decisions.
  V. To be able to properly train subordinates in the positions they are best suited for.
  VI. To be able to keep good human relations among his subordinates.
  VII. To be able to keep good human relations between his subordinates and himself and to earn their respect and trust.

THE PROFESSIONAL SUPERVISOR-EMPLOYEE RELATIONSHIP

There are two kinds of efficiency: one kind is only apparent and is produced in organizations through the exercise of mere discipline; this is but a simulation of the second, or true, efficiency which springs from spontaneous cooperation. If you are a manager, no matter how great or small your responsibility, it is your job, in the final analysis, to create and develop this involuntary cooperation among the people whom you supervise. For, no matter how powerful a combination of money, machines, and materials a company may have, this is a dead and sterile thing without a team of willing, thinking, and articulate people to guide it.

The following 21 points are presented as indicative of the exemplary basic relationship that should exist between supervisor and employee:

1. Each person wants to be liked and respected by his fellow employee and wants to be treated with consideration and respect by his superior.
2. The most competent employee will make an error. However, in a unit where good relations exist between the supervisor and his employees, tenseness and fear do not exist. Thus, errors are not hidden or covered up, and the efficiency of a unit is not impaired.

3. Subordinates resent rules, regulations, or orders that are unreasonable or unexplained.
4. Subordinates are quick to resent unfairness, harshness, injustices, and favoritism.
5. An employee will accept responsibility if he knows that he will be complimented for a job well done, and not too harshly chastised for failure; that his supervisor will check the cause of the failure, and, if it was the supervisor's fault, he will assume the blame therefore. If it was the employee's fault, his supervisor will explain the correct method or means of handling the responsibility.
6. An employee wants to receive credit for a suggestion he has made, that is used. If a suggestion cannot be used, the employee is entitled to an explanation. The supervisor should not say "no" and close the subject.
7. Fear and worry slow up a worker's ability. Poor working environment can impair his physical and mental health. A good supervisor avoids forceful methods, threats, and arguments to get a job done.
8. A forceful supervisor is able to train his employees individually and as a team, and is able to motivate them in the proper channels.
9. A mature supervisor is able to properly evaluate his subordinates and to keep them happy and satisfied.
10. A sensitive supervisor will never patronize his subordinates.
11. A worthy supervisor will respect his employees' confidences.
12. Definite and clear-cut responsibilities should be assigned to each executive.
13. Responsibility should always be coupled with corresponding authority.
14. No change should be made in the scope or responsibilities of a position without a definite understanding to that effect on the part of all persons concerned.
15. No executive or employee, occupying a single position in the organization, should be subject to definite orders from more than one source.
16. Orders should never be given to subordinates over the head of a responsible executive. Rather than do this, the officer in question should be supplanted.
17. Criticisms of subordinates should, whoever possible, be made privately, and in no case should a subordinate be criticized in the presence of executives or employees of equal or lower rank.
18. No dispute or difference between executives or employees as to authority or responsibilities should be considered too trivial for prompt and careful adjudication.
19. Promotions, wage changes, and disciplinary action should always be approved by the executive immediately superior to the one directly responsible.
20. No executive or employee should ever be required, or expected, to be at the same time an assistant to, and critic of, another.
21. Any executive whose work is subject to regular inspection should, wherever practicable, be given the assistance and facilities necessary to enable him to maintain an independent check of the quality of his work.

MINI-TEXT IN SUPERVISION, ADMINISTRATION, MANAGEMENT, AND ORGANIZATION

I. Brief Highlights

Listed concisely and sequentially are major headings and important data in the field for quick recall and review.

A. Levels of Management
Any organization of some size has several levels of management. In terms of a ladder, the levels are:

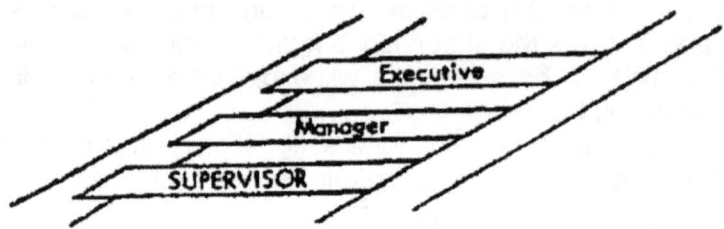

The first level is very important because it is the beginning point of management leadership.

B. What the Supervisor Must Learn
A supervisor must learn to:
1. Deal with people and their differences
2. Get the job done through people
3. Recognize the problems when they exist
4. Overcome obstacles to good performance
5. Evaluate the performance of people
6. Check his own performance in terms of accomplishment

C. A Definition of Supervisor
The term supervisor means any individual having authority, in the interests of the employer, to hire, transfer, suspend, lay-off, recall, promote, discharge, assign, reward, or discipline other employees or responsibility to direct them, or to adjust their grievances, or effectively to recommend such action, if, in connection with the foregoing, exercise of such authority is not of a merely routine or clerical nature but requires the use of independent judgment.

D. Elements of the Team Concept
What is involved in teamwork? The component parts are:
1. Members
2. A leader
3. Goals
4. Plans
5. Cooperation
6. Spirit

E. Principles of Organization
1. A team member must know what his job is.
2. Be sure that the nature and scope of a job are understood.
3. Authority and responsibility should be carefully spelled out.
4. A supervisor should be permitted to make the maximum number of decisions affecting his employees.
5. Employees should report to only one supervisor.
6. A supervisor should direct only as many employees as he can handle effectively.
7. An organization plan should be flexible.

8. Inspection and performance of work should be separate.
9. Organizational problems should receive immediate attention.
10. Assign work in line with ability and experience.

F. The Four Important Parts of Every Job
1. Inherent in every job is the *accountability* for results.
2. A second set of factors in every job is *responsibilities*.
3. Along with duties and responsibilities one must have the *authority* to act within certain limits without obtaining permission to proceed.
4. No job exists in a vacuum. The supervisor is surrounded by key *relationships*.

G. Principles of Delegation
Where work is delegated for the first time, the supervisor should think in terms of these questions:
1. Who is best qualified to do this?
2. Can an employee improve his abilities by doing this?
3. How long should an employee spend on this?
4. Are there any special problems for which he will need guidance?
5. How broad a delegation can I make?

H. Principles of Effective Communications
1. Determine the media.
2. To whom directed?
3. Identification and source authority.
4. Is communication understood?

I. Principles of Work Improvement
1. Most people usually do only the work which is assigned to them.
2. Workers are likely to fit assigned work into the time available to perform it.
3. A good workload usually stimulates output.
4. People usually do their best work when they know that results will be reviewed or inspected.
5. Employees usually feel that someone else is responsible for conditions of work, workplace layout, job methods, type of tools/equipment, and other such factors.
6. Employees are usually defensive about their job security.
7. Employees have natural resistance to change.
8. Employees can support or destroy a supervisor.
9. A supervisor usually earns the respect of his people through his personal example of diligence and efficiency.

J. Areas of Job Improvement
The areas of job improvement are quite numerous, but the most common ones which a supervisor can identify and utilize are:
1. Departmental layout
2. Flow of work
3. Workplace layout
4. Utilization of manpower
5. Work methods
6. Materials handling

7. Utilization
8. Motion economy

K. Seven Key Points in Making Improvements
1. Select the job to be improved
2. Study how it is being done now
3. Question the present method
4. Determine actions to be taken
5. Chart proposed method
6. Get approval and apply
7. Solicit worker participation

L. Corrective Techniques of Job Improvement
Specific Problems
1. Size of workload
2. Inability to meet schedules
3. Strain and fatigue
4. Improper use of men and skills
5. Waste, poor quality, unsafe conditions
6. Bottleneck conditions that hinder output
7. Poor utilization of equipment and machine
8. Efficiency and productivity of labor

General Improvement
1. Departmental layout
2. Flow of work
3. Work plan layout
4. Utilization of manpower
5. Work methods
6. Materials handling
7. Utilization of equipment
8. Motion economy

Corrective Techniques
1. Study with scale model
2. Flow chart study
3. Motion analysis
4. Comparison of units produced to standard allowance
5. Methods analysis
6. Flow chart and equipment study
7. Down time vs. running time
8. Motion analysis

M. A Planning Checklist
1. Objectives
2. Controls
3. Delegations
4. Communications
5. Resources
6. Manpower

7. Equipment
8. Supplies and materials
9. Utilization of time
10. Safety
11. Money
12. Work
13. Timing of improvements

N. Five Characteristics of Good Directions
In order to get results, directions must be:
1. Possible of accomplishment
2. Agreeable with worker interests
3. Related to mission
4. Planned and complete
5. Unmistakably clear

O. Types of Directions
1. Demands or direct orders
2. Requests
3. Suggestion or implication
4. volunteering

P. Controls
A typical listing of the overall areas in which the supervisor should establish controls might be:
1. Manpower
2. Materials
3. Quality of work
4. Quantity of work
5. Time
6. Space
7. Money
8. Methods

Q. Orienting the New Employee
1. Prepare for him
2. Welcome the new employee
3. Orientation for the job
4. Follow-up

R. Checklist for Orienting New Employees   Yes   No
1. Do you appreciate the feelings of new employees
   when they first report for work?   ___   ___
2. Are you aware of the fact that the new employee must
   make a big adjustment to his job?   ___   ___
3. Have you given him good reasons for liking the job and
   the organization?   ___   ___
4. Have you prepared for his first day on the job?   ___   ___
5. Did you welcome him cordially and make him feel needed?   ___   ___

	Yes	No

6. Did you establish rapport with him so that he feels free to talk and discuss matters with you? ___ ___
7. Did you explain his job to him and his relationship to you? ___ ___
8. Does he know that his work will be evaluated periodically on a basis that is fair and objective? ___ ___
9. Did you introduce him to his fellow workers in such a way that they are likely to accept him? ___ ___
10. Does he know what employee benefits he will receive? ___ ___
11. Does he understand the importance of being on the job and what to do if he must leave his duty station? ___ ___
12. Has he been impressed with the importance of accident prevention and safe practice? ___ ___
13. Does he generally know his way around the department? ___ ___
14. Is he under the guidance of a sponsor who will teach the right way of doing things? ___ ___
15. Do you plan to follow-up so that he will continue to adjust successfully to his job? ___ ___

S. Principles of Learning
1. Motivation
2. Demonstration or explanation
3. Practice

T. Causes of Poor Performance
1. Improper training for job
2. Wrong tools
3. Inadequate directions
4. Lack of supervisory follow-up
5. Poor communications
6. Lack of standards of performance
7. Wrong work habits
8. Low morale
9. Other

U. Four Major Steps in On-The-Job Instruction
1. Prepare the worker
2. Present the operation
3. Tryout performance
4. Follow-up

V. Employees Want Five Things
1. Security
2. Opportunity
3. Recognition
4. Inclusion
5. Expression

W. Some Don'ts in Regard to Praise
1. Don't praise a person for something he hasn't done.
2. Don't praise a person unless you can be sincere.
3. Don't be sparing in praise just because your superior withholds it from you.
4. Don't let too much time elapse between good performance and recognition of it

X. How to Gain Your Workers' Confidence
Methods of developing confidence include such things as:
1. Knowing the interests, habits, hobbies of employees
2. Admitting your own inadequacies
3. Sharing and telling of confidence in others
4. Supporting people when they are in trouble
5. Delegating matters that can be well handled
6. Being frank and straightforward about problems and working conditions
7. Encouraging others to bring their problems to you
8. Taking action on problems which impede worker progress

Y. Sources of Employee Problems
On-the-job causes might be such things as:
1. A feeling that favoritism is exercised in assignments
2. Assignment of overtime
3. An undue amount of supervision
4. Changing methods or systems
5. Stealing of ideas or trade secrets
6. Lack of interest in job
7. Threat of reduction in force
8. Ignorance or lack of communications
9. Poor equipment
10. Lack of knowing how supervisor feels toward employee
11. Shift assignments

Off-the-job problems might have to do with:
1. Health
2. Finances
3. Housing
4. Family

Z. The Supervisor's Key to Discipline
There are several key points about discipline which the supervisor should keep in mind:
1. Job discipline is one of the disciplines of life and is directed by the supervisor.
2. It is more important to correct an employee fault than to fix blame for it.
3. Employee performance is affected by problems both on the job and off.
4. Sudden or abrupt changes in behavior can be indications of important employee problems.
5. Problems should be dealt with as soon as possible after they are identified.
6. The attitude of the supervisor may have more to do with solving problems than the techniques of problem solving.
7. Correction of employee behavior should be resorted to only after the supervisor is sure that training or counseling will not be helpful.

8. Be sure to document your disciplinary actions.
9. Make sure that you are disciplining on the basis of facts rather than personal feelings.
10. Take each disciplinary step in order, being careful not to make snap judgments, or decisions based on impatience.

AA. Five Important Processes of Management
1. Planning
2. Organizing
3. Scheduling
4. Controlling
5. Motivating

BB. When the Supervisor Fails to Plan
1. Supervisor creates impression of not knowing his job
2. May lead to excessive overtime
3. Job runs itself—supervisor lacks control
4. Deadlines and appointments missed
5. Parts of the work go undone
6. Work interrupted by emergencies
7. Sets a bad example
8. Uneven workload creates peaks and valleys
9. Too much time on minor details at expense of more important tasks

CC. Fourteen General Principles of Management
1. Division of work
2. Authority and responsibility
3. Discipline
4. Unity of command
5. Unity of direction
6. Subordination of individual interest to general interest
7. Remuneration of personnel
8. Centralization
9. Scalar chain
10. Order
11. Equity
12. Stability of tenure of personnel
13. Initiative
14. Esprit de corps

DD. Change

Bringing about change is perhaps attempted more often, and yet less well understood, than anything else the supervisor does. How do people generally react to change? (People tend to resist change that is imposed upon them by other individuals or circumstances.

Change is characteristic of every situation. It is a part of every real endeavor where the efforts of people are concerned.

1. Why do people resist change?
   People may resist change because of:
   a. Fear of the unknown
   b. Implied criticism
   c. Unpleasant experiences in the past
   d. Fear of loss of status
   e. Threat to the ego
   f. Fear of loss of economic stability

2. How can we best overcome the resistance to change?
   In initiating change, take these steps:
   a. Get ready to sell
   b. Identify sources of help
   c. Anticipate objections
   d. Sell benefits
   e. Listen in depth
   f. Follow up

II. Brief Topical Summaries

   A. Who/What is the Supervisor?
      1. The supervisor is often called the "highest level employee and the lowest level manager."
      2. A supervisor is a member of both management and the work group. He acts as a bridge between the two.
      3. Most problems in supervision are in the area of human relations, or people problems.
      4. Employees expect: Respect, opportunity to learn and to advance, and a sense of belonging, and so forth.
      5. Supervisors are responsible for directing people and organizing work. Planning is of paramount importance.
      6. A position description is a set of duties and responsibilities inherent to a given position.
      7. It is important to keep the position description up-to-date and to provide each employee with his own copy.

   B. The Sociology of Work
      1. People are alike in many ways; however, each individual is unique.
      2. The supervisor is challenged in getting to know employee differences. Acquiring skills in evaluating individuals is an asset.
      3. Maintaining meaningful working relationships in the organization is of great importance.
      4. The supervisor has an obligation to help individuals to develop to their fullest potential.
      5. Job rotation on a planned basis helps to build versatility and to maintain interest and enthusiasm in work groups.
      6. Cross training (job rotation) provides backup skills.

7. The supervisor can help reduce tension by maintaining a sense of humor, providing guidance to employees, and by making reasonable and timely decisions. Employees respond favorably to working under reasonably predictable circumstances.
8. Change is characteristic of all managerial behavior. The supervisor must adjust to changes in procedures, new methods, technological changes, and to a number of new and sometimes challenging situations.
9. To overcome the natural tendency for people to resist change, the supervisor should become more skillful in initiating change.

C. Principles and Practices of Supervision
1. Employees should be required to answer to only one superior.
2. A supervisor can effectively direct only a limited number of employees, depending upon the complexity, variety, and proximity of the jobs involved.
3. The organizational chart presents the organization in graphic form. It reflects lines of authority and responsibility as well as interrelationships of units within the organization.
4. Distribution of work can be improved through an analysis using the "Work Distribution Chart."
5. The "Work Distribution Chart" reflects the division of work within a unit in understandable form.
6. When related tasks are given to an employee, he has a better chance of increasing his skills through training.
7. The individual who is given the responsibility for tasks must also be given the appropriate authority to insure adequate results.
8. The supervisor should delegate repetitive, routine work. Preparation of recurring reports, maintaining leave and attendance records are some examples.
9. Good discipline is essential to good task performance. Discipline is reflected in the actions of employees on the job in the absence of supervision.
10. Disciplinary action may have to be taken when the positive aspects of discipline have failed. Reprimand, warning, and suspension are examples of disciplinary action.
11. If a situation calls for a reprimand, be sure it is deserved and remember it is to be done in private.

D. Dynamic Leadership
1. A style is a personal method or manner of exerting influence.
2. Authoritarian leaders often see themselves as the source of power and authority.
3. The democratic leader often perceives the group as the source of authority and power.
4. Supervisors tend to do better when using the pattern of leadership that is most natural for them.
5. Social scientists suggest that the effective supervisor use the leadership style that best fits the problem or circumstances involved.
6. All four styles—telling, selling, consulting, joining—have their place. Using one does not preclude using the other at another time.

7. The theory X point of view assumes that the average person dislikes work, will avoid it whenever possible, and must be coerced to achieve organizational objectives.
8. The theory Y point of view assumes that the average person considers work to be a natural as play, and, when the individual is committed, he requires little supervision or direction to accomplish desired objectives.
9. The leader's basic assumptions concerning human behavior and human nature affect his actions, decisions, and other managerial practices.
10. Dissatisfaction among employees is often present, but difficult to isolate. The supervisor should seek to weaken dissatisfaction by keeping promises, being sincere and considerate, keeping employees informed, and so forth.
11. Constructive suggestions should be encouraged during the natural progress of the work.

E. Processes for Solving Problems
1. People find their daily tasks more meaningful and satisfying when they can improve them.
2. The causes of problems, or the key factors, are often hidden in the background. Ability to solve problems often involves the ability to isolate them from their backgrounds. There is some substance to the cliché that some persons "can't see the forest for the trees."
3. New procedures are often developed from old ones. Problems should be broken down into manageable parts. New ideas can be adapted from old one.
4. People think differently in problem-solving situations. Using a logical, patterned approach is often useful. One approach found to be useful includes these steps:
   a. Define the problem
   b. Establish objectives
   c. Get the facts
   d. Weigh and decide
   e. Take action
   f. Evaluate action

F. Training for Results
1. Participants respond best when they feel training is important to them.
2. The supervisor has responsibility for the training and development of those who report to him.
3. When training is delegated to others, great care must be exercised to insure the trainer has knowledge, aptitude, and interest for his work as a trainer.
4. Training (learning) of some type goes on continually. The most successful supervisor makes certain the learning contributes in a productive manner to operational goals.
5. New employees are particularly susceptible to training. Older employees facing new job situations require specific training, as well as having need for development and growth opportunities.
6. Training needs require continuous monitoring.
7. The training officer of an agency is a professional with a responsibility to assist supervisors in solving training problems.

16

8. Many of the self-development steps important to the supervisor's own growth are equally important to the development of peers and subordinates. Knowledge of these is important when the supervisor consults with others on development and growth opportunities.

G. Health, Safety, and Accident Prevention
1. Management-minded supervisors take appropriate measures to assist employees in maintaining health and in assuring safe practices in the work environment.
2. Effective safety training and practices help to avoid injury and accidents.
3. Safety should be a management goal. All infractions of safety which are observed should be corrected without exception.
4. Employees' safety attitude, training and instruction, provision of safe tools and equipment, supervision, and leadership are considered highly important factors which contribute to safety and which can be influenced directly by supervisors.
5. When accidents do occur, they should be investigated promptly for very important reasons, including the fact that information which is gained can be used to prevent accidents in the future.

H. Equal Employment Opportunity
1. The supervisor should endeavor to treat all employees fairly, without regard to religion, race, sex, or national origin.
2. Groups tend to reflect the attitude of the leader. Prejudice can be detected even in very subtle form. Supervisors must strive to create a feeling of mutual respect and confidence in every employee.
3. Complete utilization of all human resources is a national goal. Equitable consideration should be accorded women in the work force, minority-group members, the physically and mentally handicapped, and the older employee. The important question is: "Who can do the job?"
4. Training opportunities, recognition for performance, overtime assignments, promotional opportunities, and all other personnel actions are to be handled on an equitable basis.

I. Improving Communications
1. Communications is achieving understanding between the sender and the receiver of a message. It also means sharing information—the creation of understanding.
2. Communication is basic to all human activity. Words are means of conveying meanings; however, real meanings are in people.
3. There are very practical differences in the effectiveness of one-way, impersonal, and two-way communications. Words spoken face-to-face are better understood. Telephone conversations are effective, but lack the rapport of person-to-person exchanges. The whole person communicates.
4. Cooperation and communication in an organization go hand in hand. When there is a mutual respect between people, spelling out rules and procedures for communicating is unnecessary.
5. There are several barriers to effective communications. These include failure to listen with respect and understanding, lack of skill in feedback, and misinterpreting the meanings of words used by the speaker. It is also common

practice to listen to what we want to hear, and tune out things we do not want to hear.
6. Communication is management's chief problem. The supervisor should accept the challenge to communicate more effectively and to improve interagency and intra-agency communications.
7. The supervisor may often plan for and conduct meetings. The planning phase is critical and may determine the success or the failure of a meeting.
8. Speaking before groups usually requires extra effort. Stage fright may never disappear completely, but it can be controlled.

J. Self-Development
1. Every employee is responsible for his own self-development.
2. Toastmaster and toastmistress clubs offer opportunities to improve skills in oral communications.
3. Planning for one's own self-development is of vital importance. Supervisors know their own strengths and limitations better than anyone else.
4. Many opportunities are open to aid the supervisor in his developmental efforts, including job assignments; training opportunities, both governmental and non-governmental—to include universities and professional conferences and seminars.
5. Programmed instruction offers a means of studying at one's own rate.
6. Where difficulties may arise from a supervisor's being away from his work for training, he may participate in televised home study or correspondence courses to meet his self-development needs.

K. Teaching and Training
1. The Teaching Process
Teaching is encouraging and guiding the learning activities of students toward established goals. In most cases this process consists of five steps: preparation, presentation, summarization, evaluation, and application.

   a. Preparation
   Preparation is two-fold in nature; that of the supervisor and the employee. Preparation by the supervisor is absolutely essential to success. He must know what, when, where, how, and whom he will teach. Some of the factors that should be considered are:
   1) The objectives
   2) The materials needed
   3) The methods to be used
   4) Employee participation
   5) Employee interest
   6) Training aids
   7) Evaluation
   8) Summarization

   Employee preparation consists in preparing the employee to receive the material. Probably the most important single factor in the preparation of the employee is arousing and maintaining his interest. He must know the objectives of the training, why he is there, how the material can be used, and its importance to him.

b. Presentation
In presentation, have a carefully designed plan and follow it. The plan should be accurate and complete, yet flexible enough to meet situations as they arise. The method of presentation will be determined by the particular situation and objectives.

c. Summary
A summary should be made at the end of every training unit and program. In addition, there may be internal summaries depending on the nature of the material being taught. The important thing is that the trainee must always be able to understand how each part of the new material relates to the whole.

d. Application
The supervisor must arrange work so the employee will be given a chance to apply new knowledge or skills while the material is still clear in his mind and interest is high. The trainee does not really know whether he has learned the material until he has been given a chance to apply it. If the material is not applied, it loses most of its value.

e. Evaluation
The purpose of all training is to promote learning. To determine whether the training has been a success or failure, the supervisor must evaluate this learning.
In the broadest sense, evaluation includes all the devices, methods, skills, and techniques used by the supervisor to keep himself and the employees informed as to their progress toward the objectives they are pursuing. The extent to which the employee has mastered the knowledge, skills, and abilities, or changed his attitudes, as determined by the program objectives, is the extent to which instruction has succeeded or failed.
Evaluation should not be confined to the end of the lesson, day, or program but should be used continuously. We shall note later the way this relates to the rest of the teaching process.

2. Teaching Methods
A teaching method is a pattern of identifiable student and instructor activity used in presenting training material.
All supervisors are faced with the problem of deciding which method should be used at a given time.

a. Lecture
The lecture is direct oral presentation of material by the supervisor. The present trend is to place less emphasis on the trainer's activity and more on that of the trainee.

b. Discussion
Teaching by discussion or conference involves using questions and other techniques to arouse interest and focus attention upon certain areas, and by doing so creating a learning situation. This can be one of the most

valuable methods because it gives the employees an opportunity to express their ideas and pool their knowledge.

    c. Demonstration
The demonstration is used to teach how something works or how to do something. It can be used to show a principle or what the results of a series of actions will be. A well-staged demonstration is particularly effective because it shows proper methods of performance in a realistic manner.

    d. Performance
Performance is one of the most fundamental of all learning techniques or teaching methods. The trainee may be able to tell how a specific operation should be performed but he cannot be sure he knows how to perform the operation until he has done so.
As with all methods, there are certain advantages and disadvantages to each method.

    e. Which Method to Use
Moreover, there are other methods and techniques of teaching. It is difficult to use any method without other methods entering into it. In any learning situation, a combination of methods is usually more effective than any one method alone.

Finally, evaluation must be integrated into the other aspects of the teaching-learning process.

It must be used in the motivation of the trainees; it must be used to assist in developing understanding during the training; and it must be related to employee application of the results of training.

This is distinctly the role of the supervisor.

www.ingramcontent.com/pod-product-compliance
Lightning Source LLC
Chambersburg PA
CBHW081814300426
44116CB00014B/2352